WHAT MEAN THESE STONES?

WHAT MEAN THESE STONES?

Edited by Leonard E. Buck

The Historical Committee
Bible Fellowship Church
600 South Main Street
Coopersburg, Pennsylvania 18036

First Edition October 1983

ISBN 0-9612602-1-1

Copyright 1983

The Historical Committee
Bible Fellowship Church
600 South Main Street
Coopersburg, Pennsylvania 18036

Printed in U.S.A.

AFFECTIONATELY DEDICATED TO

Rev. C.H. Brunner

For the historical heritage
he has provided for us.
January 2, 1864 - November 20, 1949

Charles Henry Brunner was born in Hosensack, Pennsylvania. At the age of 13 he was converted and heard the call of God to the Christian ministry. He was ordained by the Mennonite Brethren in Christ Church in Allentown on February 9, 1896. It should be noted that he edited the annual yearbook of the conference for 47 years, and was also secretary of the Foreign Mission Board for 48 years. For 7 years he served as a Presiding Elder. He organized the Gospel Herald Society and served as its president from 1899 through 1905.

In 1917 the Annual Conference appointed a Hymnal Committee which included Brunner. After many meetings in the Brunner home, using pitchpipe and parlor organ, "The Rose of Sharon Hymnal was compiled. Several of the hymns were written by him.

In 1943 he retired from active work. He did not, however, go into seclusion, but served as a supply pastor on many occasions. Brother Brunner was a true servant of God and ministered to many congregations over the years. Souls were blessed by his ministry. He was a true defender of the faith and served his Lord with zeal and earnestness.

ACKNOWLEDGEMENTS

to

Rev. F. B. Hertzog
Clarence Kulp, Jr.
Raymond W. Rawn
Dorothy Brunner Wentz

and the many others
who contributed to this
Anniversary book.

Table of Contents

Introduction

1983 is a milestone in the life of the Bible Fellowship Church. This is a year to remember for this is the one hundred and twenty-fifth anniversary of the founding of our denomination. It is also the occasion of the one hundredth Annual Conference, as well as the three hundredth anniversary of the arrival of our parents, the Mennonites, to this new world of religious freedom.

In the beginning years of our denomination two conferences were held each year and minutes were recorded by two secretaries, one in English and one in German, to meet the need of a bilingual community. After a few years it was decided to have only one conference which would be known as the Annual Conference. Those early conferences, like those of today, were times of good fellowship and spiritual uplift. They were also times when church matters were discussed and principles and procedures were established, some of which have carried on to this day.

Since those early days the Bible Fellowship Church has grown to a group of fifty autonomous churches, scattered across Pennsylvania, New Jersey, New York, Delaware and Connecticut. It maintains VICTORY VALLEY, a camp for young people, and PINEBROOK BIBLE CONFERENCE, a retreat for spiritual refreshment. There is also the HOME FOR THE AGING, PINEBROOK JUNIOR COLLEGE, and an active CHURCH EXTENSION DEPARTMENT which is constantly expanding into new areas. Twelve new churches are currently being nursed to maturity. Home and foreign missionaries under THE BOARD OF FOREIGN MISSIONS are proclaiming the gospel to every creature. As we take this opportunity to look back there is only one response we can offer, to praise the Lord for His faithfulness to our generations. "Great is the Lord and greatly to be praised."

It would be impossible to present this anniversary book without some explanation of its content. On the surface it may appear to be a peculiar assortment of unrelated materials. We must admit it is a collection of unusual items; however, each one reflects an outstanding element of our church history.

The first recorded historical sketches were penned by C.H. Brunner, oft times to fill up a vacant page in the Annual Conference Journal which he edited. Unofficially he was our first church historian, and because of his writings we have a record of our beginnings. The first pages of this book present his account of the establishment of the denomination and our first church and the early camp meetings which were a part of our church life.

In 1867 the first Church Discipline was published. Today only a copy or two of this document are known to exist. It is a significant document of our past and worthy of its inclusion in this book. It is vitally important that it be reproduced for its very survival.

In the nineteenth century it was the practice of traveling evangelists and preachers to present their testimony in printed form to give credence to their ministry and witness to God's grace and saving power. As you read these stories you will walk with these men through hard places and rejoice with them in what God did as He worked miracles in their lives. These were rough diamonds in a rough age, but God continued to polish them until they became true men of God and leaders of men.

In the photo section you may look at selected pictures from the past. Some of these have never before been published.

The Historical Committee takes pleasure in presenting this unique anniversary volume.

"When your children shall ask their fathers in time to come, saying, What mean these stones? Then ye shall let your children know..."

Note: In order to preserve the true flavor of these writings the grammar and spelling of the original manuscripts have not been corrected or edited.

Retrospect
by C.H. Brunner
From the 1921 Annual Conference Journal

This Annual Conference may well be called one of the milestones in the onward march of the Pennsylvania Conference, as is seen by the reports contained in this Year Book as well as by the testimonies of those who had the privilege and pleasure to be present. Such peace and harmony prevailed from the beginning to the end so that, to say the least, we never had a better one.

This caused us to take a look backward and see where we came from. Not having any detailed official history from which to draw facts, we gathered a few fragments here and there which we trust may be of interest to our people, especially so to the younger members of our churches.

There was a young man in the Old Mennonite Church by the name of John H. Oberholtzer, who was elected as a minister in 1842. He was a man of more than ordinary attainments, holding many more advanced and liberal views of church policy than his contemporaries.

This caused a serious strain of fellowship among the conservative members of the Franconia, Montgomery County, Conference, to which the bishops and deacons of Eastern Pennsylvania belonged, resulting in the suspension of John H. Oberholtzer and a number of ministers and deacons, who held like liberal views with him, in October, 1847.

This suspension led to a separation, followed by the organization of a new society at a meeting held in Skippack, Montgomery County, on October 28, 1847, electing Elder Oberholtzer as their first Bishop.

This Society has since been known as the Conference Mennonites, designated later on in some localities as Mennonites Number Two. Among the names which appear on the records of the first meeting of this new Society we find the name of Samuel Kauffman, a deacon, the father of Abraham Kauffman, who later on became a preacher among the Evangelical Mennonites, and grandfather or our late pastor, H.A. Kauffman.

Another son of Samuel Kauffman was Milton Kauffman, for a number of years our Conference Treasurer. In a grove adjoining his farm on Chestnut Hill, near Coopersburg, Pa., our first Camp Meetings were held.

William N. Shelly was another preacher whose name appears on the records soon after the organization of the Conference Mennonites. They held their conferences semi-annually and instituted Sunday Schools in 1857. To give religious teaching to their young people, they introduced catechetical instructions.

In 1849 it was deemed necessary to select another preacher. Consequently two candidates, Samuel Stauffer, a Justice of the Peace, and William Gehman, a farmer, 22 years old, a miller by trade, were selected as candidates. Contrary to the wish of the Bishop, the lot fell upon William Gehman, who was ordained in October, 1849.

A few years later several of these families, including the above named, by the permission of the bishops, commenced to hold prayer-meetings in their homes. These were greatly blessed of God. Next year the bishops, however, revoked this privilege.

But the converting power of the grace of God had begun to operate in the community. The prayer-meetings were continued, resulting in the formation of a new body in 1853, called the Evangelical Mennonites.

At a Conference held in Flatland Meeting House on November 7, 1865, a committee, consisting of David Henning, William Gehman, Eusebius Hershey and Joseph L. Romig, was appointed to draw up a Church Discipline. From this book of 48 pages, printed by A.E. Dambly, Skippackville, Pa., in 1867, we clip the following:

"Through the convincing grace of God and the direction of several converted and pious Mennonite Preachers called of God, and a number of their members, they united themselves in the year of our Lord 1853 in order to pray with and for one another. Their number increased; many that attended the meetings became awakened and deeply convicted of their sinful condition and found peace in the wounds of Jesus.

"In order to carry on this work properly, they appointed Sabbath afternoon and evening to be spent with one another in prayer and religious exercises, prayer-meetings once a week, family worship to be held in every family as also public protracted meetings for a time, where the Word was preached every evening in purity and power.

"The number of these that attended increased and such who received the Word felt sorrow and repentance for their sins, were born again, willing to lay down a true confession before God and men and were baptized, were added to the society.

"This was the origin of the Evangelical Mennonite Society. On the 24th day of September, 1858, the first Meeting of Preachers or Conference was held, even in the private house of David Musselman in Upper Milford Township, Lehigh County, Pa., at which the following were present: Elders—William N. Shelly and William Gehmann. Preachers—David Henning and Henry Diehl. Deacons—David Gehmann, Joseph Schneider and Jacob Gottshall.

"The second meeting assembled itself on the first Tuesday of November, 1859, in the Evangelical Mennonite Meeting House in Haycock Township, Bucks County, Pa. After this two Conferences were held yearly, in June and November."

When this last named Meeting House was built we could not ascertain, but the records state that the Church at Upper Milford, now Zionsville, 36 by 50 feet, was built in 1859, the membership numbering 24. (See Journal for 1915, page 33.) So the church at Haycock may have been built about the same time.

This new body called Evangelical Mennonites soon spread into different directions and a church was built in Coopersburg, another in Quakertown, from the material of the Haycock church, and others in Springtown, Bangor, Terre Hill and other places until November 8, 1979, when a union was effected at Coopersburg with the United Mennonites of Canada and the name changed to "Evangelical United Mennonites."

From this time on the Conferences were held annually, in February or March, instead of semi-annually as before. From this date on we are having Presiding Elders, William Gehman being the first one, serving in this capacity for twelve consecutive years.

On December 27, 1883, at a Conference held in Harrisburg, Ohio, the Brethren in Christ in Ohio united with us and the present name, "Mennonite Brethren in Christ," was adopted.

At a Conference held at Zionsville, March 3-6, 1899, the time of the Annual Conference was changed from Spring to Fall and ever since they have been held about the second or third week in October.

The first Journal was published in 1896, thus making this the twenty-sixth issue. Many of the earlier issues are out of print and such who are in possession of complete sets, from the first volume published in 1896, may consider themselves fortunate.

The first Journal, an edition of 200 copies, contained 24 pages, without illustrations and very much condensed statistics. This year's volume, an edition of 925 copies, contains a large number of half-tone cuts, made from actual photographs never before published, and complete statistical tables.

The first Journal reports a membership of 720, while this one records 2183, an increase of over 200%.

A comparison of a few of the offerings may be interesting:

	Foreign Missions	Foreign Missions in S.S.	Sunday School Work	Total Receipts
1896	$ 281.56	$ 309.65	$ 589.36	$ 9,445.78
1921	10,203.25	7,953.94	13,872.24	169,726.76

Thus these annual Year Books are a record of what the Lord has done, not what we did. To Him be all the glory.

Our First Church
by C.H. Brunner
From the 1915 Annual Conference Journal

Zionsville, Pa.

The first church is located near Zionsville, Pa. The Perkiomen Railroad passes the whole length of the church yard and cemetery along the wire fence. It was formerly called Upper Milford.

Here the first congregation of the Conference was organized in the year 1853 under the name of "Evangelical Mennonites."

Here within these walls the Pennsylvania Conference held twenty-four of its sessions (most of them semi-annual up to 1879).

Here have been held two important Sessions of the General Conference, one of which was held November 8-12, 1879, at which the name was changed to Evangelical United Mennonites.

This, the first church built by the Pennsylvania Conference, was built in 1859. The contractor was Nathan Stahl. The church is 36 by 50 feet and originally had two front doors where the windows are now. The members did all the hauling free so that the church complete cost only $1200.00.

There were only a few families at the time the Church was built, aggregating about twenty-four members, among whom Father William Gehman is the only survivor. Among the heads of these families were the following:

William Gehman, who was the founder of the Conference, the father of one of our Presiding Elders and was Chairman of at least twenty-nine Sessions of the Conference. He is remarkably well preserved and present at every Conference and Camp Meeting, although almost 89 years of age. Father Gehman attended 16 Semi-Annual Conference Sessions while he was a member of the "Oberholtzer" Mennonite Conference, 43 Semi-Annual Conference Sessions of the Evangelical Mennonites, 5 Annual Conference Sessions of the Evangelical United Mennonites and 32 Annual Conference Sessions of the Mennonite Brethren in Christ. This makes a total of 96 consecutive Semi-Annual and Annual Conferences without missing one Session. Besides this he attended 7 General Conference Sessions at six of which he was a member. This makes this present Session the 103rd that he attended without intermission. He was a member of all of these Conference Sessions. Truly a remarkable record.

At this Session Father Gehman gave us a very stirring and touching address during which he remarked that after eight years of ministry in the old church under much opposition he was voted out of the Church at their regular Session at Springtown, Pa. He was a member of a Conference of forty-seven members and was expelled because he held prayer meetings. Of these forty-seven he is the only survivor.

Father Gehman said in his address: "I am like a tamed wild goose which will be content to be with the geese on the farm until in the fall when the wild geese are flying south, then you will have to clip its wings or it will fly away with the flock. I often said, 'I will not go to the next Conference,' but when the time comes you would have to clip my wings to keep me at home."

David Gehman, who was Secretary of thirty or more of their Conferences, which were held semi-annually in those days. He was also the grandfather of the present Secretary of the Annual Conference, while other grand-children and great-grand-children are ministers, ministers' wives and officers in the church. Soon after this church was built, he built a store building in Hosensack, about two miles south of the church. The second floor he arranged as a hall, put in pews, pulpit, etc., where services were held regularly for many years.

Henry Gehman, many of whose descendants down to great-great-grand-children, are active members of the church.

Jacob Musselman, father-in-law of Father William Gehman, among whose descendants some are preachers, and Foreign Missionaries.

David Musselman, the grandfather of our esteemed leaders, Presiding Elder H.B. Musselman and Missionary Presiding Elder, W.B. Musselman, and the ancestor of about a dozen ministers and missionaries.

The land, belonging to Samuel Kauffman, the great-grandfather of H.A. Kauffman, Secretary of the Gospel Herald Society, was donated free of charge.

The first funeral held in this church was that of Abraham Kauffman, the great-great-grandfather of H.A. Kauffman. He was the first person buried in the adjoining graveyard.

Here lie buried Pastors Abraham Kauffman, Joseph Romig and A.B. Gehret.
Here in the quiet church-yard are
"The mossy old graves where the pilgrims sleep."
Here
"Securely shall their ashes lie,
Waiting the summons from on high."

The Church of Our Fathers
A Short Memory Sketch
by C.H. Brunner
From the 1930 Annual Conference Journal

In these days there are many empty country churches, the members having moved to the cities and the congregations feeling unable or unwilling to continue the worship of God for which once they or their forefathers sacrificed and toiled.

Not so with the church of this sketch, situated along the highway leading from the village of Vera Cruz, Lehigh County, Pennsylvania, about one mile south. Being near to Zionsville, the church is called Zionsville M.B. in C. Church. Even though many members have moved away, services are being held here regularly summer and winter, Sunday School, preaching and the weekly prayer meeting. The present pastor is Rev. G.F. Yost, of Emaus.

Sunday, September Seventh, 1930, was observed in this church as Home Coming Day. The people gathered together from the neighborhood as well as from Emaus, Macungie, Allentown, Bethlehem, Easton, Reading, Coopersburg, Royersford, Philadelphia, and other places.

In the morning service, the Pastor of the church, Rev. G.F. Yost, preached the sermon. In the afternoon, addresses were given by the writer and also by Presiding Elder W.G. Gehman, of Easton, Pa., both of whom had been members of this congregation in their younger days. Rev. Gehman is the youngest son of the venerable late William Gehman, the founder of the congregation and also of the denomination.

In the evening, Rev. Gehman was the speaker. The attendance was very large, especially in the afternoon, half of the audience not being able to enter the church. In anticipation of this, Rev. B. Bryan Musselman, Pastor of the "Radio Church," 526-530 North Eighth Street, Allentown, Pa., installed his Public Address System, for the benefit of the overflow audience in the church yard. This gave excellent service and was very much appreciated.

During the afternoon service, Pastor Musselman read a letter of congratulation to the congregation from Rev. H.B. Musselman, Presiding Elder of the District, who was unable to be present on account of other appointments. Mrs. Amanda Wieand, the oldest member of the congregation, gave her testimony. Special singing was furnished by the Mixed Chorus and the German Mixed Quartette.

The records give the beginning of the work here several years before the first conference, which was held in 1858, making this occasion a Diamond Jubilee of praise for what God has wrought.

This church was built in 1858 under the direction and supervision of William Gehman, a young minister at that time, and a number of the pioneer members living in the neighborhood, among whom were David Musselman, Samuel Kauffman, David Gehman and others, who fell asleep many years ago. It is a simple brick structure thirty-six by fifty feet. Aside from the work contributed by the members, the building cost about $1200.00. Great forest trees were then standing in the church yard. The Perkiomen Railroad was cut through very near to the church in 1875. The original pews are still in use, although somewhat improved and arranged in three aisles and one door. The present altar, at which many penitents have bowed, has long since taken the place of the old "mourners' bench" where the fathers and mothers of many families have found their Lord. There was no recess back of the pulpit, but the words "Blessed are they that hear the word of God, and keep it" (Luke 11:28) were painted in large letters in German on the wall over the pulpit. Two oil lamps on pedestals, one at each end of the long pulpit, and several on wall brackets, and two large wood stoves, furnished the light and heat in the early years of the church.

The congregation spent hundreds of dollars during the past summer renovating the church, clearing away the old sheds, grading and beautifying the cemetery in this lovely "country church yard." This is a credit to the Board of Trustees, the class and their Pastor.

All the services, preaching and singing, of these early days and for many years had been in the German language. The Sunday School lessons were taught from a large four-page monthly paper called "Himmel's Manna," published by John G. Stauffer, of Quakertown. Jonas Y. Schultz, M.D., wrote the Sunday School notes for this paper.

Visiting preachers often came and preached for us, among whom we remember Eusebius Hershey, an itinerant evangelist, who traveled on horseback across the country, making many journeys over the Allegheny Mountains, slow and dangerous travelling in those days. He made thirteen journeys on horseback to Canada. He spent much of his early days among the Indians, preaching the Gospel to them through an interpreter, which seemed to have been one of his chief joys. He spent his last days in missionary work in Liberia, Africa, where he was buried. He had been chairman of two semi-annual conference sessions held in this church.

David Henning, of Bangor, Pa., served as chairman of seven semi-annual conferences also held in this church. William N. Shelly, uncle and great uncle of some who are now members and officers of the church, was chairman three times. William Gehman held seven of these semi-annual and two annual gatherings in the church which he has built. In all twenty-four sessions, most of them semi-annual, were held here, and also two General Conferences. Several Russian Mennonite ministers who had left their native country on account of persecution, passing through on their way to Kansas, where they took up homesteads, stopped and preached and sang in this church. We remember the name of Heinrich Emms and one by the name of Burgdorff.

The first deacon of this church, if our memory serves us correctly, was David Gehman, a merchant, living about three miles south of the church, the grandfather of the writer. William Yeakel was his successor. It seemed to have been one of the duties of the deacon to follow the sermon with a short exhortation.

William Gehman was for many years the leader of this young organization. He served many years as pastor, was chairman of seventeen conferences, held semi-annually, until 1879, and from then on he served in the same capacity at twelve annual sessions. He served locally and where called upon during his later years, preaching in power with a clear mind and voice up to the last Sunday before his death. He fell asleep in Jesus on April 12, 1918, at the age of 91 years, 2 months and 20 days.

David Musselman was another of the pioneers of this church. Before the church was built, the first conference was held in his home, about a quarter of a mile East. He was the father of Pastor Jonas Musselman, the grandfather of Presiding Elder H.B. Musselman, of Allentown, Rev. W.B. Musselman, of Cleveland, Ohio, President of the Gospel Worker Society, and the late Pastor A.B. Musselman; also the great-grandfather of Pastor B. Bryan Musselman, of Allentown. He died November 21, 1904, at the age of 96 years, 6 months and 12 days. His brother, Jacob Musselman, father-in-law of William Gehman, also was a member here.

The names of many others might be mentioned who assisted nobly in the building up of the congregation, but time and space will not permit. We will, however, mention Pastor Abraham Kauffman, whose father owned the farm of which the churchyard and cemetary originally were a part; Levi N. Shelly, another farmer living near by, whose children and grandchildren are worshipping here, some holding office in the church. We well remember the earnest prayers of these aged saints that God should bless their children and their children's children unto the generations to come. To the best of our recollection, there are about one hundred and forty descendants of three of the oldest original families now members of this and other churches in the neighborhood and throughout this and other States.

From among these pioneer families came about a score of preachers of the Gospel, minister's wives or missionaries. God did honor the "Faith of our fathers" and answer the prayers of these saints.

Here rest the remains of the grandfathers of both of our Presiding Elders and of the writer, parents, brothers and sisters and children awaiting the sounding of the last trumpet when they shall rise with bodies incorruptible and together with the living saints, will be caught up to meet the Lord and be forever with Him.

The Church and Missions

Who can tell how much the labors, sacrifices, sufferings, journeyings, preaching, prayers, and tears of these early ministers of the Gospel helped those poor lonely settlers in their homes; how many churches were organized where the revival fires burned brightly and how many of the great preachers of their time came forth through their efforts. The record of their devoted lives should help to stem the tide of worldliness, luxury and ease which is threatening the very foundations which were laid by these early messengers of the Cross.

The leading figure and founder of the Pennsylvania Conference of the Mennonite Brethren in Christ was William Gehman, of Zionsville, Lehigh County. This new Society was organized in the home of David Musselman, grandfather of W.B. Musselman, of Cleveland, Ohio, and H.B. Musselman, of Allentown, Pennsylvania, in the year 1858, about seventy-two years ago. The house where this first conference was held, near Dillinger station, is still standing. From the beginning Rev. William Gehman was recognized as the leader and was officially elected Presiding Elder from 1880 to 1891.

In 1891, Rev. W.B. Musselman was elected Presiding Elder and served until 1898. During these years he organized a band of young lady missionaries who realized a divine call for missionary work. This organization was called the Gospel Worker Society, which was later incorporated, doing Home Missionary work in tents and halls and also colportage work. This Society owns and operates a large publishing house in Cleveland, Ohio, known as the Union Gospel Press, publishing the Christian Life Series of Sunday School supplies, tracts and religious magazines.

At the Annual Conference in March, 1898, Brother W.B. Musselman expressed his call to devote his time exclusively to missionary work and asked to be relieved from his office as leader of the Church, whereupon the Conference elected C.H. Brunner, Presiding Elder. By this time, a number of young men had been expressing a call from the Lord, asking for opportunities in missionary work.

This led to the organization of the Gospel Herald Society a few months later, with C.H. Brunner, President. The Rules and Regulations adopted at that time remain fundamentally unchanged.

In 1905 the Conference elected W.G. Gehman, the youngest son of the founder of the Pennyslvania Conference, as President of the Gospel Herald Society, which office he has filled very efficiently to this date.

Through the stimulus of a number of the younger ministers of the Conference, the Church as a whole became very much interested in both the home and foreign end of the work. The Church felt that the time had come to not only strengthen the stakes but lengthen the cords also. Young men applied for work. The Church began to take new interest in their prayers and offerings for the extension of the work.

We have included in this report a financial statement of Missionary offerings which will no doubt be of great interest to all who are concerned in the work. Those who have been actively and intimately connected with this work from the beginning will know that very many of these offerings have meant real sacrifice and self-denials on the part of many of the faithful members, young and old, of our various congregations, especially so in the earlier years.

This money was used, we believe, conscientiously and economically for the opening and sustaining of new missions and in assisting weak and struggling missons in the Church. The Lord will remember and reward the labor of love, prayers and confidence which the faithful members of the older congregations as well as of the younger churches and missions have bestowed upon the work. God has been giving the increase in workers, missions and converts so that every one can feel that Missionary work is a safe and paying investment. The Secretary of the Board of Foreign Missions submits a rather elaborate Annual Report to Conference, so we feel that a word or two for our Home Missionary work in the Church as well as in the Society would be both stimulating and profitable.

The Headquarters and Literature departments of the Society are located at 1136 Northampton Street, Easton, Pa.

Although the Society has never been large numerically, it has been doing a great work all along, which "that day" shall declare.

The following pastors, now serving appointments in the Pennsylvania Conference, entered the Gospel Herald Society from various congregations in the Church where they were faithful members: F.M. Hottel, T.D. Gehret and J.B. Henry, from Bethlehem, Pa.; P.T. Stengele and Paul E. Baer, from Allentown (Bethel), Pa.; N.H. Wolf and J.B. Layne, from Philadelphia (Salem); W.F. Heffner, from Reading, Pa.; H.K. Kratz, from Hatfield, Pa. Among these also was H.A. Kauffman, from Coopersburg, Pa., who fell asleep in Jesus while untiringly ministering to his flock during the terrible Influenza epidemic of 1918.

The Pastors who came into the. Conference through the Gospel Herald Society from the Gospel Worker Society are G.F. Yost, from York, Pa.; E.E. Kublic, from Shamokin, Pa.; V.H. Reinhart, from Baltimore, Md., and E.H. Musselman, from Cleveland, Ohio.

There are also nine young men who are active members of the Gospel Herald Society who either passed the Reading Course of the Conference or are studying it now, who hold Annual Conference License.

Among the Foreign Missionaries and those who at the present time are engaged in Christian service exclusively, the names of nineteen or more could be mentioned who had been members of the Gospel Herald Society.

Adding to these the six young men who are working in the Society but are not yet licensed we have at least forty-nine young men who are today in the active work of the Church at home or abroad or in the Society, including five who died while in active service, all of whom has received training for pastoral or missionary work in the Gospel Herald Society.

The Society now maintains seven missions with a bright outlook for the future. Among the great needs are more workers and better and more suitable places of worship. Pray to this end.

The following church appointments have been turned over to the Conference from the Gospel Herald Society:

Philadelphia, Pa. (Salem), 1906. This mission was started at 2310 Germantown Avenue late in 1898 by the Gospel Herald Society. It was organized as a church in 1906. Property at Eleventh and Ontario Streets purchased, remodeled and occupied in 1907. The present church property on McFerran Street, near Broad and Pike Streets, was purchased in 1923. Present membership, 224.

Easton, Pa., 1909. This was a continuation of the work started in Phillipsburg, N.J., in 1903 by the Gospel Herald Society, but was later on moved to Twelfth Street, near Ferry Street, Easton, just a few feet from where the present church building now stands. This church was organized in 1909. Present membership, 137.

Stroudsburg, Pa., 1910. The Gospel Herald Society started in East Stroudsburg with a tent meeting in 1903. The church was organized in 1910 but was transferred permanently to Stroudsburg in 1913. Present membership, 63.

Shamokin, Pa., 1915. The work here was opened by the Gospel Worker Society and taken over by the Gospel Herald Society in 1907. The church was organized in 1915. Present membership, 140.

Sunbury, Pa., 1917. This mission was also started by the Gospel Worker Society and was taken over by the Gospel Herald Society in 1907. The church was organized in 1917. Present membership, 92.

Scranton, Pa., 1922. The work at Scranton was started by the Gospel Worker Society and transferred to the Gospel Herald Society in 1917. The church was organized in 1922. Present membership, 64.

Philadelphia (West), Pa., 1927. The Gospel Herald Society started here in 1918. The church was organized in 1927 and Wissinoming, a branch of Salem congregation, was added to it. Present membership of both places, 103.

York, Pa., 1927. This place also was opened by the Gospel Worker Society and transferred to the Gospel Herald Society in 1914 and organized as a church in 1927. Present membership, 92.

So our members and friends can feel perfectly safe in making liberal investments in this Home Mission Fund for the salvation of souls and the hastening of the Coming of the Lord. An itemized, audited financial account is published annually in the Year Book. Pray for the Gospel Heralds and their President.

Pledges for this Home Mission work are taken annually in all of our churches payable any time before September fifteenth. Any of our friends who wish to share in this privilege and blessing may send their contributions to any of our pastors or to Rev. H.B. Musselman, President of the Home Mission Fund, 1129 North Eighteenth Street, Allentown, Pa., to Rev. C.H. Brunner, Secretary, 3848 N. Park Avenue, Philadelphia, Pa., or to Rev. W.G. Gehman, 1136 Northampton Street, Easton, Pa., President of the Gospel Herald Society.

Camp Meetings
by C.H. Brunner
From the 1928 Annual Conference Journal
"Gather My saints together unto Me; those that have made a covenant with Me by sacrifice." (Ps. 50:5)

The first Camp Meeting is said to have been held in Kentucky on the banks of the Red River in 1799 by a Presbyterian and a Methodist minister. For several years these congregations held Camp Meetings together until gradually the Presbyterians withdrew and the Methodists continued.

Lorenzo Dow, an able though eccentric Methodist minister, first introduced Camp Meetings in Staffordshire, England, in 1807. Two Methodist ministers, Hugh Bourne and William Clowes, were so impressed with the advantages of this style of services that they persisted in holding them even after they were disapproved by the Wesleyan Conference in 1807, for which they were finally expelled and in 1810 founded the Primitive Methodist Church.

According to our record of Camp Meetings in the end of our Year Book their origin in the Pennsylvania Conference was the result of a Grove Meeting on Chestnut Hill, between Coopersburg and Limeport, Lehigh County, in August, 1879. In August, 1880, the first Camp Meeting was held in this grove with one large tent. This was owned and occupied by one of the pastors, Abel Strawn.

At the time our first Camp Meeting was held there were only three circuits in the Conference supplied in 1880 as follows: Zionsville and Fleetwood, Abraham Kauffman, pastor; Coopersburg and Springtown, Abel Strawn, pastor; Quakertown and Hatfield, Jonas Musselman, pastor. William Gehman was serving his second year as Presiding Elder.

A small temporary platform with a roof was erected for the speakers. Boards were staked down and rough planks laid across for seats. Lanterns and fishing torches were used for lights. A few years later a few street lamps and gasolene torches were counted a great improvement until we procured gasolene pressure lamps followed by electric lights.

A large tent was procured in which the meetings were held when it rained. Wooden stakes were driven into the ground and a plank nailed on top served as an altar. Around this altar the ground was covered with straw. When a rain threatened this was raked on a big heap and covered with a large canvas made for the purpose.

The first tents were made by the individuals and erected by them. Heavy muslin was tacked on a light portable frame, with doors on hinges and rafters for the roof and an extra inside roof canvas. For a number of years no one had floors in their tents. Some covered the ground with straw.

At these early Camp Meetings the top of an old cook stove with one or two pieces of pipe were placed on a wall of stones and mud about a foot high. Dry wood for fuel was gathered or brought along and here the cooking was done for the week. No oil or gasolene stoves, no boarding houses, no refreshment stand. A butcher and a baker were engaged to enter the grove and provide the campers with meat and bread several times a week but never on Sundays. Strangers came mostly provided with their own lunch. Preachers and friends coming from a distance were invited for meals in turn by the campers. No ice could be had so most of them dug a little hole in the ground, in which they placed a box to answer for a cellar.

During the eighteen years of Camp Meetings in this grove a man had to be secured who would haul the water used for drinking and cooking in barrels from a distance. Often old whiskey barrels were used for this purpose, often giving the water a peculiar taste. An attempt was made to dig a well but when it was almost a hundred feet deep and no water was found it was abandoned.

There were no trolley cars those days and the nearest railroad station was about four miles distant over hilly, stony, muddy roads.

In spite of all these disadvantages these annual gatherings increased rapidly in blessing, power and popularity, so that the grove and the roadways were filled with teams and fields had to be opened to accommodate them.

There were no dormitories or sleeping tents provided in those days so that those who had no tents to sleep in often slept in the large tabernacle on camp stools or on the straw. One of our deacons, the late Milton Kauffman, lived two fields' breadth away from the grove. He often had his house filled with women lodgers while the men, as many as forty, slept in the barn on the hay and straw.

About the year 1885 a few individual cottages were built by William Gehman, John B. Gehman and Joseph Preisch.

In 1893 several of the brethren, Milton Kauffman, H.M. Hottel and Thos. Hackman purchased thirty tents which they rented to the committee.

These were pioneer Camp Meeting days. Besides these inconveniences there were some persecutions and disturbances but the power of God was present and many were saved, sanctified, healed and blessed. Many of these have served the Lord and the church for many years and have fallen asleep in Jesus. Others are still living and they, their children and grand-children are today pillars in the Church, scattered far and wide.

Camp Meetings were held on Chestnut Hill annually for 18 years, the last one being held in 1897. The work was spreading. By this time twelve Camp Meetings had been held at seven other places, many of which were much more ocnvenient of access. Although "The Old Camp Ground" had become a sacred spot to many yet it was though wise to spread out into other sections of the country.

Up to the present time our records show that the Pennsylvania Conference has held 132 Camp Meetings in different places. In 1910 Mizpah Grove was opened. For five years three Camp Meetings were held there each season thus making 43 to date.

The History of Mizpah Grove
by C.H. Brunner
From the 1928 Annual Conference Journal

It is interesting to study the Record of Camp Meetings in the back part of the Year Book. Changing location from year to year was not always so satisfactory and to find suitable groves large enough for our annually enlarging Camp Meeting became a problem. With the advent of the automobile the parking also became a serious consideration.

Therefore the Annual Conference held in Allentown, Pa., October 18, 1909, authorized the Executive Board to purchase land or property for Camp Meeting purposes. After much diligent searching in the spring of 1910, the Board purchased a part of a grove from John F. Saeger and Andrew S. Keck, in Hanover Township, in what was then called East Allentown. This was later on incorporated in the City of Allentown, Pa., and was called the Fourteenth Ward. This tract was 356 feet wide and 700 feet long, along the south side of Lawrence Street, 5.72 acres for the sum of $3,159.53. Two lots of 20 feet each on the north side of Lawrence Street were also purchased from John F. Saeger for $300.00. A well was drilled 44 feet deep, giving an abundance of clear, cold water free from limestone. Cleaning the grove, building pulpit, well, etc., cost $758.42. The place was named Mizpah Grove, as Mizpah of old was a place for the gathering together of God's people for prayer and confession and victory (I Sam. 7:5, 6, 11, 12, 16).

In the spring of 1911 a brick building was erected by Schuler and Hottel, of Coopersburg, on the lot on the north side of Lawrence Street. The front part with a frontage of 26 feet and 28 feet deep was two stories high, while the rear part was 30 by 36 feet, only one story high. This cost $1,350.00 and was used for storage and restaurant purposes. $947.00 were spent for improving the grove. Special free-will offerings for the grove from the churches in the conference amounted to $4,758.70.

During 1912, Marcus Reinhart, of Emaus, built an auditorium 72 by 102 feet for $1,450.00 and $716.70 were spent for improvements.

In 1913 an additional strip 20 feet wide and 700 feet long along the south side of the grove was purchased from Andrew S. Keck for $321.40, or at the rate of $1,000.00 an acre, toward wich Mr. Keck donated $50.00. Improvements during the year amounted to $668.72.

Prior to 1914 the meals for the invited pastors and their families had always been prepared in a large tent erected for that purpose. In the spring of 1914 the Preachers' Dining Hall, a two-story brick building 22 feet 8 inches front by 34 feet deep, was erected by Schuler and Hottel at a cost of $978.21. Other improvements for the year cost $261.32. The Gospel Herald Society erected their Literature Cottage this spring.

During 1915 three losts, each 20 feet front and 120 feet deep, were purchased from John F. Saeger for $1,500.00, one on the west side of the Dining Hall and the other two on the east side, making five lots or 100 feet front. Improvements costing $271.70 were added this year. The City of Allentown purchased two full city blocks below Ellsworth Street for school purposes.

In 1916 only $282.17 were spent for improvements. The City erected a half million dollar public school building on their lot. Improvements and repairs during 1917 cost $430.11; during 1918, $705.59 and during 1919, $404.13.

During 1920 an additional 40 feet along the south side of the grove were purchased from Andrew S. Keck for $1,000.00, or at the rate of about $1,555.00 per acre. J.W. Shaw, of Quakertown, drilled our second or upper well, 72 feet deep, costing, with pump, $310.79. The improvements for the year cost $1,532.98.

In the early part of 1921 the Executive Board purchased from John F. Saeger all that tract on the east side of the lots previously purchased, 120 feet wide on the north side of Lawrence Street, 548.35 feet up to Gilmore Street, 120 feet beyond the former boundary line. Then a strip 124.35 wide and 441 feet long between the east side of Mizpah Grove and Gilmore Street to the end of our southern boundary line, 2 acres and 122.12 perches, for $4,350.00. The grove now contains a little more than 10 acres. Late in the fall an addition of 35 by 48 feet, with a basement, was built to the Dining Hall by James Dries, of Emaus, costing $2,272.39. Other improvements and repairs amounted to $1,361.15.

During 1922 a tarvia floor was put in and around the auditorium, which, together with other improvements, cost $1,775.84. Besides this, $792.06 were spent on other work in the grove.

Repairs and improvements during 1923 cost $719.28, while during 1924, $2,770.66 were spent, mostly to clean up, remove stones and stumps and build driveways for parking and purchasing lumber for tent floors.

During the great snow storms of January, 1925, the excessive accumulation of snow, sleet, rain and ice broke down the auditorium. Something had to be done. Contractor Jacob Hartman, of Bethlehem, was asked to secure plans and estimates for a new, larger and more substantial structure. Under the supervision of Mr. Hartman an auditorium of brick and steel construction, 82 feet wide between center of columns and 98 feet long, with an additional ten feet projection outside the posts, was built, seating about 2000 people. Under the same roof is a two-story brick building, to be used for storage, office and dormitory purposes.

Two brick lavatories, 20 by 24 feet each, one for men and one for women, were also constructed and fully equiped to meet the sanitary regulations of the City. For this purpose another artesian well was drilled, 100 feet deep. A concrete reservoir was built on top of the hill and an electric pump with automatic control installed to keep it filled during the time the camp is open.

These three buildings, with all their furnishings, together with the well, cost $28,332.57. Repairs during the year cost $380.17.

During 1926, through Mr. H.W. Yost the Executive Board purchased from John F. Saeger an additional tract of 20.83 acres on the north and east sides of what had been purchased before for a consideration of $10,000.00. Mizpah Grove now comprises 30.86 acres. A Public Address System was installed at a cost of $1,118.27. Additional expenditures for improvements and repairs amounted to $1,384.71.

During 1927 a lot of grading, work on driveways and incidental repairs cost $2,346.23.

During this summer of 1928 very extensive grading was done with a steam shovel, teams and dump trucks, filling up the old stone quarry, preparing road-ways and parking places for the widening of the altogether too congested tent circle northward.

We must not forget that during these 19 years many thousands of dollars worth of free labor was given in the grove and at the buildings by the ministers of the Conference and many of the laymen. This is worthy of mention.

Among the improvements and repairs in this statement are included about 62,000 feet of lumber and over 3,000 cubic feet of blocking which are used for tent floors and piled up well over the winter.

It might also be of interest to state that Radio Sending Station WCBA, owned and operated by Pastor B. Bryan Musselman, is located in and above the Auditorium with the studio located in the Allentown National Bank Building, Seventh and Hamilton Streets, Allentown, Pa. A number of services were broadcast from here during our Camp Meetings this past summer. Many messages of appreciation of these services were received by mail and telephone.

DOCTRINE OF FAITH,

AND

CHURCH DISCIPLINE

OF THE

EVANGELICAL MENNONITE

SOCIETY,

OF EAST PENNSYLVANIA.

——

WITH SUBJOINED CONSTITUTION OF THE

MISSIONARY SOCIETY.

——

PRINTED BY A. E. DAMBLY,

SKIPPACKVILLE, PA.

1867.

Doctrine of Faith and Church Discipline

of the

Evangelical Mennonite Society

of East Pennsylvania

Origin of the
Evangelical Mennonite Society

Through the convincing grace of God and the direction of several converted and pious Mennonite Preachers called of God, several of their members united themselves with them in the year of our Lord 1858, in order to pray with and for one another. Their number increased; many that attended the meetings became awakened and deeply convicted of their sinful condition, found peace in the wounds of Jesus, and were transplanted into the freedom of the children of God. In order to carry on this work properly, they appointed Sabbath afternoon and evening to be spent with one another in prayer and religious exercises, and also prayer meetings to be held once during the week, and family worship to be held in every family, as also public protracted meetings, where the Word for a time was preached every evening in purity and power, and the believers prayed for the deliverance of immortal souls; likewise sought to avoid all that which is evil and sinful, and to do that which is good, as far as God gave them strength and ability.

The humble of those, that desired to attend such meetings, soon increased. Such, that now received the Word, felt repentance and sorrow on account of their sins, that were inwardly renewed, born again, and baptized with the Holy Spirit of God, and became willing according to the will of God to lay down a true confession before God and men, upon their true faith according to God's ordinance, were baptized and added to the society. This was the origin of the Evangelical Mennonite Society, that spread itself in the eastern part of Pennsylvania. On the 24th of September, 1858, the first meeting of preachers or Conference was held, even in the private house of *David Musselman*, in Upper Milford township, Lehigh county, Pa.

Elders Present	Deacons Present	Preachers of the Word
William N. Schelly,	David Gehmann,	Present
William Gehmann,	Joseph Schneider,	David Henning,
	Jacob Gottshall,	Henry Diehl.

Here such articles of Faith and brief Rules, as were deemed necessary at this time for the small society, were now laid down.

The second Conference assembled itself on the first Tuesday in November, 1859, in the Evangelical Mennonite Meeting House, in Haycock township, Bucks county, Pa., where the following important resolution was adopted, viz:

"That every child of God, having proved himself such by his walk and conversation, shall have entire freedom to express himself according to the inspiration of the Holy Ghost."

After this two Conferences were held yearly, in June and November.

It is our earnest wish, that our society in the future may be gifted with men for office, filled with the Spirit of the Lord, because the harvest is great and the faithful laborers are few. Yea, may the Lord graciously own even our weak beginning, but operated upon by his Spirit and made according to his will, and even in richer measure pour out his Holy Spirit upon our society. Of course, if we only look to ourselves, or if we were obliged to undertake and carry through the important cause of our society in our own strength, we should have to despair, but let us look much more to the great promises of the Lord, take courage and trust to Him that He will verify His precious promises to us: Fear not, little flock, for it is your Father's good pleasure to grant you the Kingdom. Amen.

Introduction

The need of a "Doctrine of Faith and Church Discipline" was strongly felt by our society for several years already, since we believed and still believe, that they would serve our society as a benefit and blessing in extending itself, as also in the work for the welfare and salvation of immortal souls.

Accordingly, by a Conference held in Flatland Meeting House, on the 7th of November, 1865, there was a committee appointed, namely; David Henning, William Gehman, Eusebius Hershey and Joseph L. Roming, to draw up this Doctrine of Faith and Church Discipline, and to prepare it for printing.

We are obliged to make the same confession that other societies have made, that we do not possess the ability we should to do this work, and that this Doctrine of Faith and Church Discipline has been taken by the committee of our society, employed for the purpose, partly from the Doctrines of Faith of other Christian societies, and partly directly from the Holy Scriptures, simply and distinctly arranged according to the Word of God for the edification of the society, and for the benefit of all that may wish to connect themselves therewith.

Notwithstanding all the trouble of the committee, should however in the future anything, of which we have now not thought, be wanting (which we do not doubt at all) in this Doctrine of Faith and Church Discipline, we would take as a remedy God's Word in hand; for it is our sincere wish to take the simple and secure Bible way, as Christ, the Apostles, and Menno Simon have taught, in order to serve Almighty God, and in pursuance of Christian order to cooperate with all upright Christians for the upbuilding of His glorious Kingdom upon earth, according to the grace that He will in part from time to time. A sincere thankfulness to God our Almighty Father has already often raised itself in our hearts, as a small branch of the Church of Jesus Christ, that through the Spirit and Word of God we have been convinced of our deeply fallen condition and of our departure from God, and that we can say with the Apostle Paul: "Old things have passed away, all things have become new," as likewise that our society has hit upon such measures, that we have family worship, prayer meetings and the like, in which the brothers and sisters find opportunity to offer praise and thanksgiving for received benefits, in fellowship with the rest of the children of God, and to express their desires in regard to the condition of their own hearts as well as for the salvation of the whole congregation and the extension of God's Kingdom generally; for while we were yet members of different societies (which societies we consider spiritually dead), and were bound by laws and constitutions made by men, as is the case with many at the present time, whose wish is that their societies might also introduce family worship, prayer meetings and the like. But the teachers, as shepherds of the flock, will not advance, and in the case of most there is little hope for this cause, inasmuch as they are rather to be considered as mockers and scorners than defenders.

The most important that we wish to express in this introduction, is that which the Word of God teaches in regard to Church Ordinance, namely: that the Church shall consist only of genuine believers, whence it necessarily follows, that only such shall be allowed to be received into fellowship by the rite of holy baptism, as have found the true and living faith in Jesus Christ, in order that there may be: one Lord, one Faith, one Baptism, one God and Father of us all.

Jesus says: "By this all men shall see that ye are my disciples, if ye have love one for another, and he that has not love, will abide in death." Therefore let us exercise love, in order that we may possess that glory which Jesus obtained from the Father by prayer for His disciples, that we may be one as He and the Father are one. Therefore, beloved brethren, let us seek to be likeminded, unanimous, and harmonious, and may none speak or think evil of another, but implore the Lord that He may give us his spirit and zeal, to conduct the affairs of Christianity rightly to the honor of His holy name and to our own eternal welfare. Amen.

Statement of the Principal Articles
of our Common Christian Faith

1. God and the Creation of all Things.

Since it is proved in the Word of God, that without faith it is impossible to please God, because he that comes to God must believe that He is, and that He is the rewarder of those that diligently seek Him, Hebrews 11,6, we confess with out lips and believe in our hearts with all the pious, according to the Holy Scriptures, that there is only one true and living God; one eternal existence, and spirit without body, indivisible, infinite, mighty, wise and benevolent, the creator and preserver of all things visible and invisible. In this Godhead is a Trinity in one existence and might coeternal, namely: the Father, Son, and Holy Ghost. Rom. 11,36; 1 Cor. 12,6; 1 John 5,7.

2. The Fall of Man.

We believe and confess, conformably to the contents of the Holy Scriptures, that our first parents, Adam and Eve, did not remain long in that glorious state in which they were created, but that as they were seduced by the cunning and deceit of the serpent and the enmity of the devil, they broke the commandment of God, and became disobedient to their Creator, through which disobedience, sin, and through sin death has come into the world ("since we have all sinned"), which consequently has come upon all men, while all have sinned, and thereby have brought upon themselves God's wrath and condemnation.

3. Re-instatement of Man through the Promise of the Coming Christ.

In regard to the re-instatement of our first parents and their descendants, we believe and confess, that God, notwithstanding their fall, their transgression and sin, although there was no ability in them, yet did not entirely reject them, and did not wish to let them be lost eternally, but that He called them again to Himself, comforted them, and proved to them that there yet remained with Him a remedy for their reconciliation, namely: the immaculate Lamb, the Son of God, who was chosen for the purpose, before the foundation of the world, and while they were yet in Paradise, was promised for a reconciliation, redemption and salvation of them and all their descendants. John 1,29; 1 Peter 1,19.

4. Holy Ghost.

The Holy Ghost proceeds from the Father and Son as true and eternal God, in one existence, majesty and glory with the Father and Son.

5. The Coming of Christ into this World and the Reason of his Coming.

We believe and confess, that, as the time of the promise for which all the devout patriarchs so much longed and waited, had come, this previously promised Messiah, Redeemer, and Savior having proceeded from the Father,

27

was sent; that he came into the world, yea, became incarnate, that he was revealed, and that the Word became flesh. Further, we believe and confess according to the Scriptures, that, when he had ended his course and had finished his work, for which he was sent and for which he came into the world, according to the providence of God, he was delivered into the hands of the uprighteous, that he suffered under the ruler Pontius Pilate, was crucified, died, was buried, on the third day rose from the dead, ascended into Heaven, and that he sits on the right had of the Majesty of God, whence he will come again to judge the living and the dead. 1 Tim. 2,16; John 1,14; Luke 23,33.

6. Sufficiency of the Holy Scriptures for our Instruction in the Ways of Salvation.

We believe and confess also, that the Holy Scriptures contain the counsel of God, as far as it is necessary for us to know it for our salvation, indeed, that nothing which is not contained therein and which cannot be pointed out therefrom, can be made binding on a person as an article of faith, or as a doctrine, which he must receive and believe necessary in order to be saved.

The Holy Scriptures we understand to consist of those Canonical Books of the Old and of the New Testament, which at all times have been received in the Church without any doubt as such. John 15,15.

7. Repentance and Amelioration of Life

We believe, since the meditation of the human heart from childhood is evil, and therefore inclines to all unrighteousness, sin, and wickedness, that for this reason the first lesson of the precious New Testament of the Son of God, is repentance and amelioration of life. Therefore men must bring forth fruits meet for repentance, must ameliorate their lives, must believe the Gospel; for neither Baptism, the Lord's Supper, Church Membership, nor any other outward ceremonies, without faith, regeneration change or newness of life, can help us to please God, or to obtain consolation or promise of salvation from Him. Gen. 8,21; Mark 1,15; Gal. 6,15.

8. Holy Baptism.

Of Holy Baptism we confess, that all repentant believers, who are united to God by faith, regeneration and renewing of the Holy Ghost, and whose names are written in Heaven, upon such scriptural confession of faith and renewal of life according to the command and teaching of Christ, and according to the example and custom of the Apostles, in the exalted name of the Father, the Son and the Holy Ghost, must be baptized in water to the burial of their sins, and through the same must be united with the congregation of saints. Further, we believe in regard to baptism as Menno Simon teaches in his Articles of Faith, page 37, 38 and 39; Acts 2,38; Mat. 28,29,20.

9. Church of Christ.

We believe and confess that there is a visible Church fo Christ, consisting of those who, in the appointed way, repent rightly, believe rightly, and who are baptized, united with God in Heaven, and rightly admitted into the Congregation of Saints here upon earth. 1 Cor. 12; 1 Peter 2,9.

10. Teachers and Ministers in the Church.

We believe and confess that the Church without office and ordinance cannot continue in its growth and culture; that for this reason Christ the Lord himself, as a father in his house, has instituted his offices and ordinances, that he has given commands and injunctions concerning them, and has ordained how each one should walk therein, and have regard to his word and calling.

Further, we believe that the calling of Christian preachers and ministers happens in two ways: the godly and the ecclesiastical. Some without any interposition of man are called of God only, as was the case with the Prophets and Apostles; and some by the interposition of the pious, as may be seen in Acts 1,14. Gal. 15,16.

11. Breaking of Bread or Lord's Supper

We confess or hold, likewise, such a breaking of bread, as the Lord Jesus Christ before his suffering instituted with bread and wine, and made us of with his Apostles with whom he ate, which he commanded them to observe in remembrance of Him, his suffering and his death, and that his worthy body was broken, and his precious blood was shed for us and the whole human race. Luke 22,19,20. Acts 2,46.

12. The Washing of the Feet of the Saints.

We confess feet washing of the Saints which the Lord Jesus has instituted and commanded, who also himself washed the feet of the Apostles, and who has therefore given an example that we should likewise wash one another's feet. John 13,4, until verse 17.

13. Marriage or the Matrimonial State.

We confess in the Church of God such honorable marriage of two believing persons, as God at first in Paradise ordained, and Himself instituted between Adam and Eve. Gen. 1,27; 1 Cor. 7,39.

14. Secular Government

We also believe, that God has ordained and instituted power and government for the punishment of the evil and for the protection of the good; for this reason we do not despise them, violate or resist them, but we consider government as a servant of God, are subject and obedient to it, particularly in that which does not militate against the law, will, and commandments of God; we pay tribute and custom faithfully, and pray the Lord for its welfare, that we may live under its protection and lead a still and quiet life of Godliness and honesty. Rom. 13,1-7; Matt. 17,27; 1 Tim. 2,1-3.

15 Resistance.

As far as vengeance is concerned, by which an enemy is resisted with the sword, we believe and confess that the Lord Jesus has forbidden his disciples and followers to show vengeance and resistance, that he has commanded them not to return evil for evil, or curse for curse; but to sheathe the sword, as the Prophets foretold, to make coulters of them. Further, we believe that war and blood shedding are not conformable to the teaching of the Gospel of Christ. Matt. 5,39-45; Rom. 12,14.

16. Oaths.

Of the oath we believe that Christ likewise has forbidden his own to swear in any manner at all, but that he has commanded them that their communications should be yea, yea, and nay, nay. Hence we understand that oaths of every kind are forbidden, and that in place of them, all our promises, words and obligations, yea, all our declarations or testimonies of anything whatsoever, should be established by our word, yea, in that which is affirmed, and nay, in that which is denied. Matt. 5,34-37; 2 Cor. 1,17.

17. Excommunication, or Separation from the Church.

We believe and confess an excommunication, a separation and Christian punishment in the Church, for amendment and not for hurt, that the pure may be separated from the impure. If any one, after he has become enlightend, has accepted the knowledge of truth, and has beceome united in the society of the holy, falls into such unfruitful works of darkness whereby he is separated from God, and the Kingdom of God is denied him, such person, when his deeds are manifest and made known to the Church, shall not remain in the congregation of the righteous, but shall and must be separated as a bad member and open sinner, must be put out, and in the presence of all must be punished and swept out as a leaven, until he amends. 1 Cor. 5; 1 Tim. 5,20.

18. Shunning of the Excommunicated.

We believe and confess that when any one, either through his evil life or perverse teaching, has so far sunken that he is separated from God, consequently also excommunicated from the Church and punished, the same, according to the teaching of Christ and his apostles, without distinction, must be avoided and shunned in his unfruitful works of darkness by all co-partners and members of the congregation, and must be considered as a Gentile and Publican; however, he must not be held as an enemy, but he must be admonished, that he may be brought in such a way to a knowledge of, sorrow for, and lamentation over his sins, in order that he may again be reconciled to his God, and His Church, and consequently may again be received into the Church. 1 Cor. 5,9-11; 2 Thess. 8,14.

19. Resurrection of the Dead, and the Final Judgement.

We believe, according to the Scriptures, that through the incomprehensible power of God, on the last day all persons who have fallen asleep will be again awakened, made alive, and capable of arising, and that these, together with those that then will remain in life, in the twinkling of an eye, at the last trump, will be changed, and placed before the judgment seat of Christ; and that the good and evil will be separated from one another, and that the good or pious, as blessed, will be accepted by Christ, that they will enter upon eternal life and receive joy such as neither eye hath seen, nor ear heard nor yet entered into the heart of man; that, on the contrary, the wicked or evil, as accursed, will be cast out and banished into outer darkness, yea, into the eternal torment of hell, where the worm dieth not and the fire is not quenched. John 5, 28,19

General Rules
and
Appointed Duties of the Society

Admission of Members.

In this Society only such persons are allowed to be admitted as in the light of God have acknowledged themselves sinners, have brought forth fruits meet for repentance, have received forgiveness of their sins through faith in the precious merits of Jesus Christ, and have been baptized according to the eighth article of the Doctrine of Faith. Acts. 2, 38,41.

Of Marrying.

Corruption may be seen in Christian societies in reference to marriage. When believers marry unconverted persons the consequence is that in most cases they lay in their way a great obstacle to their salvation, and, it is to be feared, some for their whole life time. If, however, any one of our fellow members, regardless of this, ventures to marry an unconverted person, the former shall be on probation for one year.

Dress.

Although we are convinced that our carriage in the plainest way possible can save no person, if he does not put on the garment of salvation and the coat of righteousness, through Christ, yet it is also undeniable that all unbecoming ornaments of clothing are not suitable for true Christians, and in order that every one of our fellow members may know it, be it proclaimed, that no one shall be allowed to make use of the following personal ornaments, to wit: Hoops, Women's Hats, Feathers on Bonnets, Ear and Finger Rings, Powdering of the Hair, Ribbon Bows, and Moustaches, and everything that is worn for pride and conformation to the world. 1 Pet. 3,3; Rom. 12,2.

Dealing in, and Using Intoxicating Liquor.

No one of our fellow members shall be permitted to make or prepare ardent or intoxicating liquors, to deal in them, or use them as a beverage, except as a medicine. Eph. 5,18; Habakuk 3,15.

Slavery.

We have long been convinced that slavery in all its forms is a great evil and ought to be shunned by every Christian, therefore be it made known to all our fellow members that no one, under any pretence or condition, shall be allowed to hold slaves, to deal in them, or to defend slavery. Ex. 21,16; 1 Tim. 1,10.

Swearing.

Decreed: that we do not justify swearing, according to direction. Matt. 5,33-37; James 5,12.

Government.

It is required of each fellow member of this Society to be subject to all government which has power, so long as it ordains nothing which militates against the teaching of Christ; to give custom to whom custom is due, tribute to whom tribute is due, fear and honor to whom they are due, according to the Scriptures, to pray for it and to honor it; also for protection to invoke it as a servant of God, but only when it is necessary; on the contrary, in all cases in which it can be shown that it has been misused for dishonorable and wicked purposes a punishment shall follow in the Society. Rom. 13,1-7; Titus 3,1; 1 Peter 2,17.

Inoffensiveness.

It is ordained that in the Evangelical Mennonite Society it is forbidden to take the sword in order to carry on war, because we believe that only the sword of the Spirit, which is the Word of God, is given to believers for defence, Matt. 26,51.

Classes: Hours of Instruction, and How Conducted.

In order that it may be better known whether the different members of our Society have an earnest to work out their soul's salvation, the Society is divided into small companies, which we call classes. Each class consists of a number of fellow members, who shall assemble publicly at least once a week; and it is the duty of the Preachers and Deacons, as frequently as possible, to attend the classes or prayer meetings, and to conduct them according to Scriptural order; yet the same privilege shall be given to each common brother at each time.

All the members of our Society shall endeavor to lead a Godly life, be diligent in prayer—particulary in secret—and, where it is possible, to attend for their own edification all our meetings of Divine Service; to hold family devotions with their own, morning and evening, and to set a good example in all Christian virtues. Act 8,1; chap. 12,18; chap. 16,13; 1 Tim. 2,8; Col. 3,16.

Officers

Of Offices in General

Art. 1. The offices of this Society are of three kinds, viz:
First: The office of Elders.
Second: The office of ordinary Preachers, or Teachers.
Third: The office of Overseers or Deacons.

Art. 2. No one can be chosen Elder unless he is blameless, the husband of one wife, sober, temperate, well behaved, given to hospitality, apt to teach, not given to wine, no striker, not engaged in any dishonorable business.

Art. 3. No one can be chosen to conduct the ordinary service of the Word of God unless he receives good testimony of the majority of his congregation or congregations in which he shall be elected; and as the Elders must be chosen from the number of ordinary Ministers it is particularly necessary to have regard to the capability of those that shall be elected, according to 2 Tim. 2-24.

Art. 4. Decrees that as many Overseers, or Deacons, shall be in each congregation as shall be deemed necessary, who must be such men (as far as the congregation can ascertain) as are described Acts 6,3; 1 Tim. 3,7.

Election of Ministers in General.

Art. 1. From two persons who possess such abilities as have been enumerated in Section 1, Article 2, an Elder shall be chosen by lot, or if no two persons, acknowledged to be able, are at hand, the congregation or congregations, by a majority of votes, may elect one of the congregation or congregations, who is acknowledged to be able, according to Acts 1,23; chap. 5,6.

Art. 2. If any one receive an extraordinary call—that is, when any one feels himself urged by a call from God to preach—by agreement of the congregation he shall have permission to do so, yet he shall be on probation for one year before he be ordained.

Art. 3. Decrees that the ordinary Ministers of the Word of God shall be chosen in the following way and manner, namely: When the congregation or congregations have become unanimous to elect a Minister or Preacher, then shall a Minister of the Word, before voting is entered upon, remind the congregation particularly of the importance of the Ministry and see that throughout regard may be had to the Gospel, to elect no one that is not qualified to teach, but such an one that at least possesses good faculties, such as a clear and distinct voice, natural oratory, but above all, to look upon a blameless life (2 Tim. 2,24), and then prayerfully to nominate such, after which the congregation shall hold an election of those nominated, and those two who shall have received a plurality of votes shall draw lots, and he upon whom the lot falls shall be willingly accepted by the whole congregation as a Minister of the Word, ordained of God.

Art. 4. No ordinary Minister or Deacon shall be ordained or installed in office unless he answers in truth and sincerity the following two questions affirmatively:

Question 1. Are you acquainted with our Doctrine of Faith and Church Discipline?

Question 2. Will you follow and defend them?

Art. 5. When any one is elected to the office of Elder, another Elder shall install him in office with the laying on of hands. 2 Tim. 2,2; John 21,17.

Art. 6. When any one is elected to the ordinary Ministry, according to order given in Arts. 2 and 3, an Elder shall (and if an Elder be not at hand, another ordinary Minister shall) install in the office of common Ministry the newly elected one, by agreement of the congregation in which the newly elected shall serve.

Art. 7. Deacons or Almoners, can be chosen by lot or elected publicly in the congregation, as a vote of two-thirds may decide, yet in every case regard must be had to the integrity and piety of the person or persons nominated.

Art. 8. Determines that an ordinary Minister may install in office an elected Deacon by agreement of the congregation in which the newly elected shall serve.

Duties of Officers.

Art. 1. The Duties of an Elder are to continue in prayer, to proclaim the Word of God in purity and sincerity, to exercise reason among those who are obedient to the faith, orderly to administer baptism and the Lord's Supper according to the intention of Christ, to watch over the ordinary Ministers as well as the Deacons and congregation or congregations, to become acquainted with those who have trusted their souls to his guardianship in order that at the proper time he may give each one his due, and to teach and practice nothing except that which agrees strictly with the doctrine of Christ. It is his duty, in conjunction with the ordinary Ministers and Deacons, or by their consent, (as also by agreement of the congregation in many cases when its counsel is necessary) to enforce and exercise Christian order in his congregations, according to the doctrine of the Gospel. He shall be a pattern to believers, in word, in behavior, in spirit, in faith, in purity. He shall persevere in reading, in admonishing, in teaching, and shall not disregard the gift that is given him through prophecy and the laying on of hands of the Elders. He shall attend to and practice these, that in all things he may increase and that his increase may be manifest. He shall take care of himself and of the doctrine of the Gospel, and persevere in these particulars, that he may cause himself and those who hear him to be saved.

Art. 2. The duties of an ordinary Minister of the Word of God are in every case to support the Elder, so far as the Elder will discharge the duties of his office according to the doctrine of the Gospel, and as far as he is in need of his assistance. Act. 16,9.

Art. 3. No ordinary Minister, as well as no Deacon, can be employed by an Elder for service unless they are unanimous in doctrine, life and faith. 2 Cor. 6,14-16.

Art. 4. The ordinary Ministers, or the Deacons, shall be allowed to discharge all the duties of the different offices, yet only in cases of necessity shall they be permitted to administer the breaking of bread or the Lord's Supper.

Art. 5. At all times the counsel and consent of a congregation are called for when anything of importance shall be undertaken and transacted in it.

Art. 6. An ordinary Minister in every particular shall be obliged and shall have the same right, according to his spiritual ability, to discharge the same duties of office that are made incumbent on the Elder, except the exercise of those high duties that are pointed out in the 4th Article under Section 3, that all things may always be done in order.

Art. 7. Makes it the duty of the Deacons to attend Divine Service as regularly as it is possible for them, for support and encouragement of their Ministers; to visit the sick and to encourage them in their sufferings, according to their spiritual ability, to take courage in the conflict, to infuse Christian resignation into them and to comfort them; also to make inquiry in regard to the poor and suffering members in their congregations and to care that they may receive assistance and alleviation, to such an extent as the congregation may deem necessary. Acts 6.

Art. 8. Grants the right to the Deacons to receive all the money that is given by the congregation for the poor, according to their best to give conscientiously to the needy, and in every such case to proceed as the circumstances may call for.

Art. 9. It is also the duty of the Deacon to see that there is always order in the congregation; he shall also inform his fellow ministers, or the congregation, without any delay, when he discovers anything which threatens danger to the congregation, that soon counsel may be taken in regard to it, and that a right watchful eye may be had upon the doctrine and Church of Christ, as is becomming.

Art. 10. When a Minister in an orderly way is once called to the Ministry of the Gospel and has obligated himself to defend, to support and to teach the principles, in the manner which our Society requires, according to the teaching of Christ, he is bound all his lifetime to continue in the Ministry of the sanctuary; for this reason, he cannot be allowed to devote himself to any secular calling by which he neglects the duties of his office. Therefore it is a prime duty of those who have received the benefits of his services, or his spiritual gifts, to allow him to receive something of their temporal gifts—that is, when the Minister finds himself in such circumstances that he must neglect his duties, which are manifold, in order to gain a livelihood. 1 Cor. 9,14; Gal. 6,6.

Art. 11. Decrees that the Minister dare not, on any account, proclaim the Gospel for the sake of any worldly gain; else his reward will be in vain, since he makes Godliness a trade. He must so act as if he had not the least to expect in return, altogether out of love to God and his neighbor. But when those who have received the benefit of his services do not in return show love towards the needy Minister, love must cease, and little can be built up or improved. The mere wish of luck and blessing cannot save the needy one from his want. James 2,16; Matt. 10,8-10.

Conference.

Art. 1. The sitting of the Conference shall be held semi-annually.

Art. 2. Divine Service shall be held publicly in the forenoon of the day appointed for the sitting of the Conference.

Art. 3. There shall be a President and a Secretary. These shall be elected by a majority of the members of the Conference only for one sitting, yet by their agreement shall be eligible again.

Art. 4. It shall be the duty of the President to open the meeting with singing and prayer, and then to hold the election to choose a President and a Secretary.

Art. 5. The official and moral conduct of the Preachers and Deacons shall be examined.

Art. 6. It shall be the duty of the Secretary to enter all the transactions of the Conference in a book.

Art. 7. The members of the Conference shall only be engaged in such matters that aim at the welfare and edification of this Society, as well as of the kingdom of Jesus Christ generally.

Missionary Cause of the
Evangelical Mennonite Society

The Preachers, Deacons, and all the members shall be considered to take an active part in the Missionary cause, and, as circumstances will allow, to establish missions here and there; hence it shall be the duty of each Conference to assign each Missionary his field of labor; and every commissioned Missionary from time to time shall present to the Conference an accurate report of his work, his travels, and also of his receipts and expenditures, as the constitution of our Missionary Society prescribes.

Marriage Formula

Question 1. Are you still resolved to enter into the state of holy matrimony with this woman standing by your side? If this is still your desire, then in the presence of God and these witnesses answer, *Yes.*

Are you still resolved to enter into the state of holy matrimony with this man standing by your side? If this is still your desire, then in the presence of God and these witnesses answer, *Yes.*

Question 2. Do you confess that you are free, unmarried, and loose from all other women, as far as the state of matrimony is concerned? If you can sincerely confess this before God and us all, then answer, *Yes.*

Do you confess that you are free, unmarried, and loose from all other men, as far as the state of matrimony is concerned? If you can confess this before God and us all, then answer, *Yes.*

Question 3. Will you take this woman for your wife, to live with her in holy matrimony according to God's ordinance; will you love, comfort, and honor her, in good as well as in evil report, rich or poor, keep and maintain her in sickness as well as in health, and forsaking all others cleave to her alone, and that so long until death shall separate you? If you will do this, then answer, *Yes.*

Will you take this man for your husband, to live with him in holy matrimony, according to God's ordinance; will you render obedience to him, and be ready to serve, love, and honor him, in good as well as in evil report, rich or poor, administer to him in sickness as well as in health, and forsaking all others cleave to him alone, and that so long until death shall separate you? If you will do this, then answer, *Yes.*

4. Then the Preacher kneeling down will pray with the wedding couple.

5. After they have arisen from prayer, the preacher will join the right hands of both, and say: "What God has joined together, let no man put asunder," and bless them in holy wedlock in the name of the Father, the Son, and the Holy Ghost.—Amen.

Art. 1. When any one in some way has offended against purity of doctrine or of life, and this offence is not generally known, the offender shall only be privately admonished. If the offender, who has only been once admonished by some one, shows sorrow, he shall be pardoned; if not, he shall again be admonished in the presence of two or three witnesses; and if yet no sorrow follows, he shall be reported to the Congregation; and if he will not heed the Congregation, such an impenitent sinner must be treated according to the precept of Jesus. Matt. 18.

Art. 2. Any member of the Congregation who defends such an impenitent and ecommunicated member stands in danger of receiving the same fate, inasmuch as he is to be considered as if he took part in his evil deeds.

Art. 3. If, however, this excommunicated member return and give infallible proof of sincere sorrow and unfeigned repentance, he shall again be admitted by agreement of the Congregation.

Art. 4. If, however, the crime be so shocking that a toleration of it would be a shame and scandal to the Congregation and the religion of Jesus Christ, the officers of the Congregation shall hold a council in regard to such a member, and, immediately after his guilt be made manifest, he shall be separated from the Congregation, so that the evil may be put out from it, according to 1 Cor. 5,1-13.

Art. 5. The following crimes and vices must be excluded, viz: False doctrine, blasphemy, litigiousness, false witness, perjury, theft, fornication, adultery, lying, drunkenness, quarreling, malice, fraud, violence, unjust gain, wantonness, violation of the Sabbath, impudent mockery, cruelty to inferiors, and the like.

Art. 6. Shows that when an Elder, ordinary Minister, or Deacon has become guilty of such a crime the Congregation shall authorize some one to investigate the matter without delay; and, in case the matter be confirmed, he shall be suspended until the sitting of the next Conference; if the accused cannot free himself then, and if he will show no sincere sorrow, to the satisfaction of the Congregation, he shall be deposed from his office until he manifest sincere and unfeigned repentance.

Art. 7. The Apostolic precepts and these regulations demand that always at least two witnesses by necessary, and indeed such as command respect, to prove an officer guilty of any crime. 1 Tim. 5,19.

Art. 8. Decrees that no one of our Preachers shall be allowed to marry unconverted persons, and particularly no one shall be allowed to marry a couple when the one party is converted, or is a true believer, and the other is unconverted, or is a disbeliever, since it cannot be done in the Lord, as the Apostle Paul teaches it should. 1 Cor. 7,9.

Art. 9. Decrees that all transgressions, matters in dispute, or dissensions that arise in a Congregation, shall always be corrected in the Congregation in which they originate, after they have been investigated by the Deacon of the Congregation, and the transgressor admonished. Matt. 18,15-17; 1 Cor. 5,13.

Art. 10. Decrees that persons wishing to be admitted into our Society as members, in the presence of God and men shall answer sincerely the following four questions, namely:

Question 1. Have you obtained peace with God, through forgiveness of your sins, by faith in Jesus?

Question 2. Have you the Spirit of God that bears witness with your spirit that you are a child of God?

Question 3. Are you acquainted with our Doctrine of Faith and Church Discipline?

Question 4. Will you follow and defend them?

Art. 11. Decrees that our fellow members are not allowed to be connected with secret societies.

Art. 12. Decrees that at any time an addition may be made to these regulations, but not except by agreement of two-thirds of the members of the Conference.

Art. 13. No article, or part of it, which these regulations contain shall be altered or annulled, except by the consent of two-thirds of the members of the Conference.

Art. 14. Decrees that the officers who justify these regulations shall subscribe their own names thereto.

Elders	Preachers	Deacons
David Henning	Henry Diehl	David Gehman
William Gehman	Abel Strawn	Joseph Schneider
Eusebius Hershey	John Musselman	Aaron Unangst
William N. Schelly	Abraham Kauffman	
	Joseph L. Romig	

Constitution

of the

Missionary Society

We, as a small branch of the Christian Church, feel in duty bound to render obedience to the precepts of our Lord and Savior, who offered up his life out of love towards us, in order to redeem us from eternal death; since he has commanded his Apostles, as well as all who love him, to go into all the world, to preach the Gospel to every creature, (Mark 16,15,) and to preach repentance and remission of sins among all nations, (Luke 24,47,) we, as a small division of the Mennonite Society feel it also our duty to organize a Missionary Society to contribute our mite to the great work of our Lord. May the Lord grant willing hearts and open hands, besides his rich blessing.

Art. 1. This society shall be called "The Home and Foreign Missionary Society of the Evangelical Mennonite Society of East Pennsylvania." The aim of it shall be to hit upon such measures, by contributions and means of prayer, that the kingdom of Christ may be extended by Missionaries.

Art. 2. Every Congregation shall organize a Missionary Class, and the Preacher or Deacon shall hold a Missionary meeting every three months, and every member of our Society, quarterly, shall voluntarily contribute a certain sum for its support, according as the Lord has blessed him. Also, members of other confessions may join such Classes to assist in advancing the work of the Lord.

Art. 3. The society shall hold a yearly meeting, a short time before the Spring sitting of the semi-annual Conference, to elect officers for the society, and to transact other business; on which occasion a Missionary sermon shall be preached and a public collection shall be held for the benefit of the Missionary cause.

Art. 4. The officers of this society shall be a President, a Secretary, and a Treasurer, who shall all be members of the Evangelical Mennonite Society, and shall be elected annually; by its agreement, however, they shall be eligible again.

Art. 5. Every Congregation or Missionary Class shall elect a Secretary and a Treasurer for a term of three years. The duty of the Secretary shall be to keep a book in which he shall enter the names of the members opposit to their contributions. The Treasurer shall receive all contributions paid in and shall annually pay them over to the chief Treasurer of the Society.

Art. 6. It shall be the duty of the President to see that the regulations of the Constitution be observed in all respects, and to preside over the yearly meeting and all business meetings; in case, however, the President be absent, deceased or deposed from his office, the Secretary shall take his place.

Art. 7. The Secretary shall take note of all the transactions of the Society and transcribe them in a register, shall record the amounts collected which at each meeting are handed in to the Treasurer, and keep an account of other contributions to the society. In case the offices of the President and Secretary have become vacant, their duties shall devolve upon the Treasurer, until their places be filled by an election at an annual meeting. Should the office of the Treasurer become vacant, the President shall appoint a person to fill the vacancy until an annual meeting of the Society. Should it become necessary at any time for the Secretary to take the place of the President, he may appoint himself an assistant.

Art. 8. The Treasurer of the Society shall receive all moneys of the class Treasurers, and all bequest or presents given for the society, and shall keep a book in which he shall enter punctually all the receipts of the society; both he and the Secretary, every time after a lapse of six months, shall present their books at the sitting of the semi-annual Conference, and exhibit an accurate account of their receipts and expenditures.

Art. 9. Every Preacher who has been commissioned as a Missionary by the Council shall present to the Conference an accurate report of his travels and labors, and of his receipts and expenditures, semi-annually or annually, as he shall be called upon, and the Conference shall then grant an order of the Treasurer in his favor, specifying the amount he shall pay him out of the Treasury.

Art. 10. At any time an addition or amendment may be made to this Constitution by agreement of two-thirds of the Council members.

Signed by the President and Secretary of the Conference.

Life Experiences of
William K. Ellinger, Traveling Preacher

William K. Ellinger was born July 8, 1838 - date of his death is unknown to us. He lived in the area of the Perkiomen Creek near Skippack and in Phila- delphia. He was a traveling preacher when we were known as The Evangel- ical Mennonites.

Now walk through the pages of Ellinger's experiences and marvel how any one man could get into so much trouble. His old life without Christ is a graphic testimony of "the wages of sin." Then God reached out and gave him a new life.

Editor

This record of my life is not prompted by any feeling of vain-glory, or any craving for notoriety; neither is it because I have had a very remarkable history; but having been a great sinner, and having found Jesus a great Saviour, I would tell my story that others may be led to seek and adore the blessed Friend who has saved, and thus far kept, me by His grace.

I was born in the State of Pennyslvania, Montgomery County, near Jefferson- ville, July 8th, 1838.

My father was a blacksmith by trade, and an honest man, and worked hard to provide a comfortable living for his family. He accumulated some money and moved to Skippackville, and from there to the Trappe, and from this place to a place at the mouth of Perkiomen and North East Branch Creek, about one mile from Schweneksville, and three miles from Zeiglersville. This place my father bought for $1,500. It was a beautiful place of twenty-nine acres, with a large house, a carpenter shop and a blacksmith shop. Here he worked at his trade and attended the farm, and provided well for his family. But several years after this he quit his trade and commenced to keep tavern, and sell intoxicating drinks.

Now my dear father began to get enemies and into law troubles, which cost him a great deal of money. The devil is in this business; and all the money he earned by hard work went to the devil! All men take warning! My father lost his place because of sin, for Jesus says:

For judgement I am come into this world, that they which see not might see; and that they which see might be made blind.
And some of the Pharisees which were with him heard these words, and said unto him, Are we blind also?
Jesus said unto them, If ye were blind, ye should have no sin; but now ye say, We see; therefore your sin remaineth.—John ix, 39-41.

My father was once a Christian. He had been a member of the German Baptists or Dunkards, and he lived a consistent Christian life. I remember when he and my mother were baptized in Perkiomen creek, when there were probably thousands of people present.

We had meetings two or three times a week in our house and barn. Father was a good man then. He had family prayer three times a day, and would teach us all to pray. He was good and kind to us then, and very seldom whipped us; but unfortunately he met a stumbling-block in his way and fell!

He was one night at John Crater's mill, when a poor man by the name of Wilson came along, and said he wanted to buy a wagon on one year's credit, but could get no security. My father promised to stand for security if the other brothers would help in case of need, and some of the Christian(?) brothers said if Wilson should fail to meet the debt they would not allow my father to pay all. The year expired and Wilson was not able to pay; my father stated the case to the other brothers, but they told him they would not pay one cent! So my father paid it all.

From this time my father began to neglect the church and prayer-meetings, and family worship, and finally he quit them all. He began to curse and swear and get cross and whip us, and finally he became one of the worst of skeptics.

I shall never forget one day my brother Henry said to Me: "Father did wrong to leave the Dunkards. He is no longer good to us. I cannot stand it much longer, he is so cross to-us."

God help us to be true Christians and faithful to God and one another, so that our brother will not stumble over us.

My father began to apply his mind to the Bible and infidelity, and he studied the Bible dilligently, and went to camp meetings and condemned the Bible and Christians. Once us boys got into a fight with the Christian boys, and got the best of them; we were nearly locked up, but we ran off the ground and went home.

There were nine children of us—seven boys and two girls.

My father was very severe with us; he did not spare the rod on his children, but this did me no good.

When I was twelve years of age my brother Henry and I ran away from home, and went to my uncle's place on the Susquehanna River, a distance of 130 miles west. We remained here a short time, and then went nine miles further up the river to work on a new railroad. Henry became a wheeler on the road, he being fifteen years old, while I was but twelve, and too small to handle a wheelbarrow, so the boss made me "jigger boy," to give out the liquor to the men, each man receiving sixteen drinks a day.

I soon learned the ropes among the boys and men.

The men would get us boys to fight one another, and I was called a fighting boy because I could master them, from six to ten in number. All of them would often get at me. And on one occasion I resorted to stones, and used them so freely that they were compelled to leave the field, and I hurt two of them so badly that my brother and I had to leave without pay.

44

From here we commenced to walk home, a distance of 139 mile, without one cent in our pockets. Over hills and mountains, through valleys and over rivers, through forests and the hot sun and dust, barefooted and footsore, so that the blood came from the soles of our feet; hungry and thirsty, sometimes for days without anything to eat but berries; at night no place to sleep but the forest, or some hay-stack or barn; the wolves howling in the mountains and hills. "The way of the transgressor is hard."

And he said, A certain man had two sons:
And the younger of them said to his father, Father, give me the portion of goods that falleth to me. And he divided unto him his living.
And not many days after the younger son gathered all together, and took his journey into a far country, and there wasted his substance with riotous living.
And when he had spent all, there arose a mighty famine in that land; and he began to be in want.
And he went and joined himself to a citizen of that country; and he sent him into his fields to feed swine.
And he would fain have filled his belly with the husks that the swine did eat; and no man gave unto him.
And when he came to himself, he said, How many hired servants of my father's have bread enough to spare, and I perish with hunger!
I will arise and go to my father, and will say unto him, Father, I have sinned against heaven, and before thee,
And am no more worthy to be called thy son: make me as one of thy hired servants.—Luke xv: 11-19.

We came across two men driving cattle, and they were going as far as Gilbertsville, within about 12 miles of my father's place. Now we got 25 cents a day and board. It took us about three weeks to get home.

We came home at twelve o'clock, midnight, and slept in the barn. In the morning our brothers came out to feed the cattle, and found us in the haymow asleep, and with great astonishment they ran in and told father. He came out rejoicing, because "These, my sons, were dead, and are alive again; they were lost, and are found." And they began to be merry, because they were all glad.

Father told us to come in and eat our breakfasts and drink our coffee, and be merry; and he said, "Be not afraid of me, I will not whip you. I am glad you are home. We thought you were dead. Do not leave us again. Boys, I was in trouble all the time about you. I would go out every night and look up and down the road to see if my dear boys were coming home. Your mother had given you up for dead, but I have never given you up entirely."

We were home awhile, then went to learn shoemaking, but we both ran away from our places, and I went to work on a farm for a man by the name of Charles Corson, for six dollars a month. This man liked me, and said he never had a better boy on his place. I remained here nine months.

I now went to learn blacksmithing with a man by the name of C. Long, at a place four miles above Greenville. He was a good man. I would not stay.

I left him and went out to a place at Greenlane to work at cigars, (a trade I picked up at my uncle's). I earned some money, and went out West with my brother Henry, to Indianapolis (750 miles from home.) We both got work on farms. Henry worked for a man by the name of Pugh, for thirteen dollars a month, and I for a man by the name of Johnston, for ten dollars a month. We were one mile apart.

My employer was a mean man, and poor pay; so I left him the first week, but could not find another place.

My brother would not leave his place, and I had not money enough to take me home, so I went to Indianapolis, to the depot, and told the president of the road a pitiful story about myself and he sent me home free of charge.

I was home only a short time, and then I went out to the same place again, and got work with a man by the name of Simon McCray for thirteen dollars per month. While here I saved enough money to buy myself forty acres of land, for one hundred dollars, on the Yellow River, and sold it for one hundred and fifty dollars, and came to Indianapolis, where I was robbed of it, but I caught the thief and got my money back, and let him go free.

And, behold, a certain lawyer stood up, and tempted him, saying, Master, what shall I do to inherit eternal life?

He said unto him, What is written in the law? how readest thou?

And he answering said, Thou shalt love the Lord thy God with all they heart, and with all thy soul, and with all thy strength, and with all they mind; and they neighbor as thyself.

And he said unto him, Thou has answered right; this do and thou, shalt live.

But he, willing to justify himself, said unto Jesus, And who is my neighbor?

And Jesus answering said, A certain man went down from Jerusalem to Jericho, and fell among thieves, which stripped him of his raiment, and wounded him, and departed, leaving him half dead.

And by chance there came down a certain priest that way: and when he saw him he passed by on the other side.

And likewise a Levite, when he was at the place, came and looked on him, and passed by on the other side.

But a certain Samaritan, as he journeyed, came where he was; and when he saw him, he had compassion on him.

And went to him and bound up his wounds, pouring oil and wine, and set him on his own beast, and brought him to an inn, and took care of him.

And on the morrow when he departed, he took out two pence, and gave them to the host, and said unto him, Take care of him; and whatsoever thou spendest more, when I come again, I will repay thee.

Which now of these three, thinkest thou, was neighbor unto him that fell among the thieves?

And he said, He that showed mercy on him. Then said Jesus unto him, Go, and do thou likewise.—Luke x: 25-37.

When I got home again I enlisted in the regular army as a cavalryman, and was sent to Carlisle barracks to be drilled to fight the Indians.

While I was in the army a number of us were accused falsely, and for punishment were ordered to carry about 120 pounds of stone in our knapsacks, and because of this unjust punishment we lay a plan to escape, and I was chosen leader. The plan proved successful, as you will see.

We were in the guard house. At three o'clock in the morning I sawed off the bars in the windows, and we passed the guards and made our escape. We slept in the woods during the day and traveled at night, when we would rob the spring-houses for something to eat. There were six of us, and we all reached home safely.

My father once more welcomed his lost son home, safe and sound.

I was not home long, however, when I was arrested and taken back in irons.

They put me in the guard-house and fastened ball and chain to me, and in this way I was compelled to work every day, with two guards armed with carbines and revolvers, watching over me while I split wood for the officers' mess. I was kept in this way for two months or more, till Jefferson Davis, then Secretary of War, pardoned me and fifteen others, and we went to our respective regiments.

When I came out of the army I lived a rambling life, traveling from one place to another.

One day I came home, and in company with my brothers got into more trouble. We were crossing some land that belonged to two brothers by the name of Tison, when they came out and commenced to club us, but we got the best of them, and they laid in their beds two weeks.

Warrants were issued, and we were arrested, tried, convicted and sentenced. My brother Jacob got four and I got six months in prison.

This was no place for us; it did us no good. We slept all the time. It was a school to make men worse. I served out my time here, although we could have got out if we had desired to do so, because I had made a key out of a meat bone to fit our door, and could unlock it, but we had only a short time to stay and did not desire to get out.

About this time the rebellion broke out, and I enlisted in Colonel Small's regiment, Washington Guards, being the third man on the roll.

On the 19th of April, 1861, our regiment, in company with the Sixth Massachusetts, and a company of Allen Rifles of Allentown, Pa., and one battery of artillery, also from Pennsylvania, reached Baltimore, and were attacked by the Baltimore rioters.

I was wounded in this battle, but I never left a battle-field, until I left my mark. Here I was compelled to kill a rebel, after which I was wounded and taken prisoner, and sent home to Philadelphia with five hundred more. After we were paroled we reached home, and I was confined to my bed for some time. When I recovered I enlisted for three years, and served through the whole war.

I was wounded several times; was a prisoner of war; was one of the men who helped to take the flag of the 34th North Carolina Infantry, at which time the whole rebel regiment were taken prisoners. On another occasion a battery of six guns, and the breast works, were taken by us. I was also a Union spy, and captured a rebel spy by the name of Reeves, in Washington City. He was tried before General Mansfield and found guilty, and was sent to Fort Lafayette, Boston harbor, for fifteen years. But when the war was over he was pardoned.

After I came home I got into a fight and was stabbed in the breast. I was carried home supposed to be dead, and I promised God—if there was a God—that if I recovered I would try to get out of this bad company and do good.

But I soon got into trouble again, and was stabbed six times and almost died, but again recovered; then I got into another fight, when I almost killed an officer and was compelled to leave the State to avoid the law. I went to West Virginia, and while I was there the difficulty was settled; but it cost me five hundred dollars.

I returned to Philadelphia and joined the volunteer fire department. The members of our company would arm themselves with revolvers and muskets, cut short so they could conceal them beneath their coats, and we would lay in the market until the members of another company would come within range, when we would fire upon them. Fortunately no one was killed.

About this time we had some trouble with the city police, who were democrats. I was chief of about twenty-five deputy marshals, appointed to enforce the election laws at the polls.

A man from Baltimore came to the polls and voted the democratic ticket. We arrested him and took him to the police station, but he was allowed to pass out of another door. We arrested him again and took him to the marshall's office, but when we got there we found it closed, and we concluded to take the prisoner to the U.S. navy yard.

On our way to the navy yard a crowd of ruffians, about two hundred in number, attempted to release the prisoner, but we were well armed, and succeeded in keeping them at bay until we got the prisoner locked up.

We then went home to our headquarters at my brother's tavern, 807 South Front Street, below Catharine, reaching there about ten o'clock at night, when most of the men went home.

About twelve o'clock, when everybody had gone home, a company of about twenty-eight officers came in to arrest us. We demanded their warrants to be shown; they refused, because they had none. We refused to go, and a battle commenced between four brothers and twenty-eight officers; which lasted about half an hour. All the glassware, window-glass and mirrors were smashed; the bar was broken into splinters; the gas was turned out; blood streamed from the heads of men on both sides, but we were overpowered, and taken into custody. There were some men hiding in an alley waiting to kill us, but their hearts failed them.

We were put in the police station, and in the morning taken before an alderman, and from there to prison. We were suffering terribly with our wounds bleeding and neglected. We got a speedy trial and were cleared.

48

Seek ye the Lord while he may be found, call ye upon him while he is near:

Let the wicked forsake his way, and the unrighteous man his thoughts: and let him return unto the Lord, and he will have mercy upon him; and to our God, for he will abundantly pardon.

For my thoughts are not your thoughts, neither are your ways my ways, saith the Lord.

For as the heavens are higher than the earth, so are my ways higher than your ways, and my thoughts than your thoughts.

For as the rain cometh down, and the snow from heaven, and returneth not thither, but watereth the earth and maketh it bring forth and bud, that it may give seed to the sower, and bread to the eater:

So shall my word be that goeth forth out of my mouth; it shall not return unto me void, but it shall accomplish that which I please, and it shall prosper in the thing whereto I sent it.

For ye shall go out with joy, and be led forth with peace; the mountains and the hills shall break forth before you into singing and all the trees of the field shall clap their hands.

Instead of the thorn shall come up the fir tree, and instead of the brier shall come up the myrtle tree; and it shall be to the Lord for a name, for an everlasting sign that shall not be cut off.—Isaiah lv: 6-13.

About this time one of my brothers had an illicit distillery back of the Shiffler hose house, and he was making money fast. He had a silent partner by the name of C———M———, who was very rich. My brother soon got quite rich and opened a tavern.

We were all engaged in politics and run the whole first ward. We were fighting men and fast voters, and smart in the business, and had the friendship of all the officers.

One night my brother Joseph, who was not interested in the still, came home from his work at the navy yard, and it being very late he slept in a wagon in the yard in company with a man who was helping to run the still, which was "going" on inside. About twelve o'clock the revenue officers came on the ground and arrested my brother Joseph and the guilty man, and tore out the still.

At this time I was night watchman in the navy yard, and when I came home in the morning and heard the news, we went up to the police station where they were locked up till a warrant and reinforcements were secured. We told the prisoners to run away when they were brought out of the cell, which they did, when the officers commenced to fire upon them, but my brothers Jacob and James, and myself held the officers by their coats till one of the prisoners got away, but the twelve revenue officers were reinforced by fifty police officers, and we were overpowered and all four of us locked up in one cell.

The officers were afraid to take us out of the station house because we had not been disarmed, and, besides, there were thousands of sympathizing friends supported by the liquor traffic, ready to rescue us. So they sent for a company of U.S. marines. They handcuffed all four of us together and marched us to the marshal's office, and from there to prison with a guard of one hundred marines and twelve revenue officers.

We were in prison about ten days when we were all bailed out. The bail was eighty thousand dollars, but had it been ten times as much we would have got it.

We were all tried at court and got clear of the charge.

Come unto me, all ye that labor and are heavy laden, and I will give you rest.

Take my yoke upon you, and learn of me; for I am meek and lowly in heart; and ye shall find rest unto your souls.

For my yoke is easy, and my burden is light.—Matt. xi: 28-30.

I now got into more trouble. I was mistaken for another man and shot at three times, being wounded in the legs and head, and left for dead. They carried me home on a stretcher. The doctor and others expressed doubts about my recovery.

O, how my soul was troubled during that sickness! I had ample time to think of my past life. As a man hungry and thirsty, upon a high mountain, with a view of comfort, food and water in the valley below him, so was I upon a mountain of sin, wounded body and soul by the devil and my sins; and the devil telling me, "You can't become a Christian; you're too big a sinner; God will not receive you."

It was a long time before I was able to come down from that mountain. Sinners, take warning from a friend; there is a hell that I passed through upon that bed of sickness. My memory became strong, so that I could remember all that I had done throughout my whole life. O, what grief I suffered!

While I was in this condition, a spirit told me that I could make a promise; and, there and then, I promised God faithfully, that I would do better if I got well. I did get well, but I carry some bullets to the grave that are still in me. I thank God that He permitted me to get well.

If a man promises God anything, God will surely hold him to his word. A man may promise another a sum of money, and when the time is come, hide from his creditor, and send a false message to him, and finally cheat him out of the debt; but you cannot hide away from God. If you attempt it He will make it warm for you as He did for Adam and Eve, in the Garden of Eden, when the Lord God called unto Adam and said unto him, "Where art thou?"

A short time after this I was afflicted with bleeding of the lungs. One night I was standing at a graveyard bleeding, and an officer took me home. I sent for a friend, thinking that I would die, but I partly recovered.

One day three of us went out gunning, and I became so heart-sick on account of my sins, that I refused to return home with the others, and I walked down the railroad and sat down awhile, and rose up and walked home more miserable than ever. So great was the conviction that was upon me, that I thought I would die. I tried every worldly means to get rid of my trouble. I went out West among the Indians and half-breeds, but my misery went with me; I prayed to the sun, moon and stars, thinking they were the great gods, and I remember once finding myself in the woods rolling amongst the briers, wrestling hard to find God! Sometimes I thought I could hear him say: "Keep up your courage, I will come in due time and meet you. When you make the right start, I will come more than half way. Get at the work right. Let my Son be your Saviour." This conviction was upon me for nearly two years.

I came home to Philadelphia from the West as bad as I was before I went. But I was bound to find God or die.

About this time I heard of some hard cases being converted at the M.E. Mariners' Bethel Church, down town, (Third St. and Washington Avenue), and I said: "If these men can find God I guess I can, too."

I went to the church three nights, and came away angered because I believed that some one had told the minister all about me, so he could preach at me.

On the third night, after the meeting was over, I made up my mind that I would give myself to the blessed Lord on the fourth night!

The next morning, when I went out, I said to myself: "I will walk straight to-day, and the Lord will receive me." But I got beastly drunk, and got into a fight. My effort was like that of a man who took a horse to the blacksmith to be shod, and wanted to do half the work to save half the cost. He commenced to drive nails in the horse's foot: the points of the nails, however, did not come out, but the blood did, and the horse kicked him to death. God pity the poor man that tries to save himself. If this could be done, God could have kept his Son at home, and we could do without a Saviour. There would be no need for him to die on the cross if a man could save himself. I see it all plainly enough now. We must come to him just as we are, with all our sores and filthy rags, and He will make us better, and give us new hearts, and make us new men and women. God help us to see it!

When night came I went to the church just as I was, and on the way to the church the devil would say to me: "Why man, you're crazy, going to church drunk! They will smell the liquor on you and run you out, and have you locked up in the station house." But this old devil did not tell me this IN THE MORNING, WHEN I WENT IN THE FIRST TAVERN AND GOT THE FIRST DRINK.

When I reached the church, I heard the sweet sound of God's love, from the hymn they were singing:—

> Dear Jesus receive me,
> No more will I grieve thee,
> Now blessed Redeemer,
> O save me at the cross.

I was brought to the floor by the power of the Holy Ghost, which Jesus sent me. I was in a trance for some time, and when I returned to consciousness, I realized fully, that I was a poor miserable undone wretch, fit only for hell. I felt so miserable and wretched, that I was tempted to kill myself, but dare not resolve upon such a course, even if I had time to do it; but there I was, in a place which I will never forget. O sinner, look and live; for why will ye die? I cried with all my might: "God be merciful to me a sinner!" And now, like a mighty rushing wind, came the rolling wave of mercy and salvation, and I was free! My eyes were opened! My ears were unstopped! and my heart was filled with love for all men, and a holy zeal for the salvation of poor sinners! God help me to be wise, and true to the heavenly inspiration of that hour!

My conversion took place in February, 1877, as near as I can recollect.

I did not remain long with this church, because as soon as I was saved, I knew I must follow Jesus, and I read in the New Testament:

Then cometh Jesus from Galilee to Jordon unto John, to be baptized of him.
But John forbade him, saying, I have need to be baptized of thee, and comest thou to me?
And Jesus answering said unto him, Suffer it to be so now; for thus it becometh us to fulfill all righteousness. Then he suffered him.
And Jesus, when he was baptized, went up straightway out of the water: and, lo, the heavens were opened unto him, and he saw the Spirit of God descending like a dove, and lighting upon him:
And lo a voice from heaven, saving, This is my beloved Son, in whom I am well pleased. Matt iii: 13-17

I joined another church called the Free Methodists, but they had the same kind of a sprinkling-pot, and I told them several times about Jesus being baptized in the river, which displeased them, and they told me that I could get baptized in some other church and still be a member of theirs. But the time came when the Lord led me out of the Free Methodists' church to a holy people, called the Evangelical United Mennonites. With these people I got baptized. These good people baptize in the river, wash feet, and do all the Bible requires us to do. If any church people read this book, I would urge them to recognize baptism by immersion, as the example of Jesus.

Since I have been a Christian, I have been laboring amongst poor perishing sinners, and God has worked through me all the time. I have been instrumental in bringing about two hundred souls to God, and inducing over four hundred men to sign the pledge, and most of them are apparently faithful to this day. But I give God the glory.

I was an exhorter in the M. E. Church, and also in the Free Methodist Church, and am now a traveling preacher in the faith of Evangelical United Mennonites. Here I am growing in the spirit, and am ready to pray with the sick, and help them under any and all circumstances. It makes no difference to me whether it is a case of yellow fever, cholera, black vomit or small pox; I am ready to go to them and help them. If the Catholic priests can go I can.

At one time six of our family had the small pox, and we went to the hospital; while here I labored amongst the sick and dying. I prayed with one man who had carried the flag of his country, and he died happy. There were also two others who found Jesus and died happy. Several others got converted. Glory to God! To Him the glory belongs.

After this I was called to Bethlehem, Pennsylvania, as a volunteer nurse, when the small pox was raging in that district, and I labored there for several months, day and night, with marked success. The suffering there was fearful. Nine persons were converted here. Glory to God!

Since I have been a Christian, I have had great temptations. I have been poor and without work, and the last meal on the table, and my wife has said "What will we do for the next?"

I said, "God will direct us," and God did provide for us every time.

Sometimes the devil would say, "If I was in your circumstances, I would go and make and sell whiskey." But I resisted.

One time a man came and offered me sixty dollars a month and board, if I would make and sell liquor for him. But I said: "Devil, get thee behind me, I know you, I'll starve before I'll do that."

One morning I started out with twenty-five cents in my pocket, and I met with a poor woman in confinement. Her husband drank hard and did no work, but I knew the condition of the woman, and gave her the twenty-five cents. God remembered me for it; for before night a man gave me two dollars for about one hour's work; and he said "I know you work for God at all times; take this, and may God help you to go about and do good to poor perishing sinners of this city, and if you get short of funds, call on me and I will help you." Glory to God!

At one time I was working at the U.S. Custom House, where there were about eighty men employed, most all of them sinners. Some of them were hard cases, and fighting men, and they knew, also, that I was at one time a man that feared neither man or devil, and that I was now a changed man.

Among them was a man by the name of Miller, who was an unbeliever. He began to taunt me about the Christians, saying there were no Christians, and that Christ was nothing more than a man, and that all the Christians were fools and devils. I listened to him for awhile and then spoke. Said I, "Mr. Miller, you child of the devil, you have known me about twenty years; you know all about me; I have been in hundreds of fights and brawls; I have made whiskey and sold it; I gambled; I cursed and swore day and night; I made money and I spent it; I got into trouble and got out of it; I have shot and stabbed men, but they all got well except one, and he was a rebel in Baltimore; I was shot and stabbed, and on a dying bed several times; I was a walking devil, and everybody was afraid of me; I served the devil faithfully, but he was a hard master and bad pay, and I was going to hell fast, where you are going, if you do not repent. You know when I was a sinner I got along poorly, because I spent my money for whiskey; but since I have become a Christian I am getting along well, am I not?"

He said, "Yes."

"Are you getting along as well as I am?"

He said, "No."

"Do you get as much money as I do?"

He said, "Yes."

"Have you as large a family as I have?"

He said, "No."

"Well, then, how is it you don't get along as well as I do?"

He said, "I spend my money for whiskey."

"Well, so did I at one time. Is your master strong enough to keep you from drinking?"

He said, "No."

"Well, my Master is. There was a time when you would not have dared to talk to me as you have this hour, but I will forgive you."

"You say you don't believe in a God. Well, I do, and you have insulted my God, and I will pray that he will come to you inside of four months, and show you himself and his power to make you believe in Him, and all the men in this place shall know it."

He said, "How will He come?"

I said, "I do not know; but to hard sinners He comes in a way that is hard. It takes a hard diamond to cut hard glass."

He said, "Well, we'll see."

The gospel was preached that day to those men as it never was preached to them before, and they will not be likely to forget it as long as they live.

When the four months were up, a woman came to the office and called me out and said that her husband (Mr. Miller,) was dying at the hospital, at Tenth and Filbert streets, and that he wanted to see me. All the men heard what she said, and there was a death-like look on all their faces. I went back and got one of the worst men among them as a witness, and we went out to see him.

When we reached the hospital Mr. Miller appeared to by dying, and he said to me:

"Give me your hand and forgive me; I have done you wrong."

I said, "That's all right; but you must ask God to forgive you." And he did, and he got well in a few days. His family were in want at this time, and I started a subscription for them, thus being enabled to return good for evil. That man became a Christian.

One time I was down to North-east Maryland, at a camp-meeting, and God was working through me wonderfully, for the salvation of sinners.

After the camp-meeting was over, they told me that there was a man in that neighborhood so bad that everybody was afraid of him. They told me that one time he wanted to bury his child in a dung pile, but the neighbors interfered.

They told me he had two sevenshooter carbines, one of them always prepared to shoot people who trespassed upon his land. He had also a large bloodhound, fastened so that no one could pass him and reach the house.

One morning I felt the Spirit prompting me to go over and see him. I told the minister and a man by the name of Steward, and the latter went along with me.

When we came to the house, the bloodhound came out like a lion, but I put my hand out in the name of the Lord, and the dog laid down in his box. We went to the door, and the lady came out and was astonished at our presence on account of the dog. The man had gone to the city, and there was no one home but the mother and daughter. We told her that we had come to pray with them. When we had prayed they were both converted.

I prevailed on her to promise that she would send her children to the Sunday School, and that she would pray three times a day, and teach the children to pray, and go to church herself, if it cost her her life. She promised faithfully, and she kept her promise.

About a month after that I heard she was one of the strongest Christians in the church, but her husband was beating her all the time.

I went down on my knees and told God all about it. I said, "God, my Saviour, will you help this woman? Her husband is an unbeliever and a bad man. Help this sister in Jesus. Amen."

The Spirit came to me and directed me to write him a letter, as follows:—

15th day of the month.

"If you don't stop, God will come on the 15th of next month at three o'clock, and give you such an overhauling that you will believe that my God hears my prayers, and will teach you that he is God over you."

The 15th of the next month came, and I received the following information: On the day and hour mentioned in the above letter, this man and his 15-year-old boy were out in the field with a two-horse wagon loading rails, when a whirlwind came and scattered the rails from the wagon, the horses ran away, and he fell off the wagon, and broke two of his ribs and two toes, and hurt his shoulder severely. He was carried home cursing and swearing that if he ever saw me he would kill me.

This man had never seen me and I had never seen him. He was not at home when we were at his house.

The people had heard of the message I sent him, and were watching its fulfillment, and when the event happened on the very minute it was predicted, they were astonished.

Rev. Joseph Travis, who was then traveling chairman of the Free Methodist Conference, came through the State of Maryland at that time, and told me the facts as recorded here.

The man got well and was kind to his wife.

One night, about two months after he got hurt, I got a dispatch through the Spirit to go down and see this man. I went and told my minister, and he advised me not to go, but I said, "I must go, and I will go."

When I got into the car, there was a man seated in front of me, and the Spirit directed me to open my Bible, which I did, and pointed out a passage for him to read, which he read; he looked at me surprised, and I said to him. "You are rich and you have land, but you are an unbeliever, and a very bad man, and if you don't give yourself to God you will lose all and die a poor, miserable sinner, and go to hell."

He looked at me and said: "Who are you and where are you going?"

I told him I was going to North-east, Maryland.

He said: "Who do you know there?"

I said: "I am going down there to see a man by the name of Curtis."

"Why that is me," said he. "What do you want with me?"

I said, "My name is Ellinger."

He said, "Is this Ellinger? I said, one time, I would kill you, but I feel different about it now. You are a man of God. Come home with me to my house and stay a month."

I went to his house and staid there one week. He treated me like a brother, and on Sunday he went to church for the first time.

The family wept. The minister said he had no leader, and directed me to fill his place, which I did. I preached about ten minutes and then began a prayer-meeting. Mr. Curtis came to the altar and was converted. The congregation wept, they were so glad. He is a Christian now.

The Midnight Robber
by Pastor C. H. Brunner

This story of David and Sarah Musselman was recorded by C.H. Brunner and takes place in January, 1883.

David Musselman lived from 1807 to 1903. He was one of the first members of our denomination and actively engaged in its establishment and ministry. It was in David Musselman's stone farmhouse that a group of men first met to organize the denomination. He later moved to another farm where our story takes place.

Editor

On a little farm near the village of Vera Cruz in eastern Pennsylvania, lived an aged couple all alone in quiet retirement. Their humble though comfortable home was situated a little distance away from the busy public thoroughfare. The house was surrounded by fruit trees of every description. Back of the house was a garden beyond which the woodland commenced reaching up to the top of the hill.

There, at this beautiful shady spot, away from the noise and rush of daily travel, these aged saints lived for many years.

More than half of their long and happy lives they had spent in the service of the Lord. They had been among the first converts in a revival which had spread throughout the community.

During these days of spiritual awakening this couple, David Musselman and his wife, together with about a dozen others organized themselves into a little congregation and built a large brick church about a mile from their home.

Here they found their greatest joy in regularly occupying a prominent place in the work and worship of the Lord.

They held their family worship regularly, the aged father reading from the big family Bible every evening before retiring, after which they both knelt down and committed their bodies and souls, house and possessions, as well as their two sons and their families, unto God for His protection.

They had victoriously stood many tests and passed through many deep waters and the God in whom they trusted had upheld them.

One cold night in the month of January in 1883, after reading their Bible and committing themselves to their great Protector as usual, the aged couple, now past the three score and ten years allotted to man, retired for the night.

During the night they were suddenly awakened out of their sound sleep, and to their surprise they saw a tall man standing a few feet away from their bed with a red handkerchief tied over his face, all but the eyes, and an ax in his hand.

Grandmother, calm and composed, lifted up her head and said to the man, "Where do you come from?" and when he did not answer she asked him, "What do you want?" Upon this the burglar stepped up to the side of the bed and lifting up his ax ready to strike, said, "I want your money and that at once. There are four more downstairs and if you don't give me your money I will call them up and we will kill you."

While this robber was standing in front of them with his uplifted ax, they heard a peculiar rushing noise as the sound of a whirlwind which filled their souls with a sweet quietness and peace and a sense of His Divine protection. They realized that the Lord of Hosts had, as it were, sent a detachment of His Heavenly hosts for their bodyguard.

By this time they both sat up in bed, and Grandmother said to him, "Don't strike; you cannot strike. Our God is stronger than you. You are alone. That is not true that there are four others downstairs. You cannot strike us." As she said this the burglar's arms dropped and he put his ax on the floor without saying a word. Then Grandmother got out of bed and took the man by the arm and preached a powerful sermon to him while he stood motionless and confounded, listening with deathly silence.

After she was done with her admonition and had exhorted him to quit his life of sin and get converted, she said to Grandfather, "We'll give him a few dollars." So Grandfather got his purse out of his trousers hanging on the bed post, took out a number of bills, and handed the ruffian a two-dollar bill.

It seemed the Lord had completely unnerved this robber by this time and had divested him of his daring boldness so that he stood there, helpless, his arm apparently paralyzed, unable even to reach out and take the money handed to him by Grandfather, so Grandmother took the money and put it into his hand saying, "Here take this."

Grandfather leisurely put the rest of his money back into the purse and put the purse into the pocket of his trousers in the presence of the robber as though it had been an ordinary business transaction.

So completely had the Lord taken all fear away from them that Grandmother even took hold of his handkerchief which he had tied over his face, to see who he was.

When the man had put the money into his pocket, he started to go downstairs, when Grandmother said, "Wait, I will take the light and light you down to the door."

As they were going downstairs she asked him, "Where did you get in?" to which he replied, "Why here through the window." Then she said, "Well you can go out through the door." and after another exhortation she opened the front door and left him out.

By this time Grandfather had dressed and come downstairs, too, and went out with him as far as the gate, opening from the yard into the lane, leading down to the main thoroughfare.

After he had watched the robber going down the lane as far as he could see him, he returned back into the house. They did not sound an alarm but both went back to bed but for joy they could not sleep the rest of the night, as they meditated upon the wondrous love and care bestowed upon them by their Heavenly Father in whom they had trusted these many years.

They spent the night in talking of what Darius said to Daniel when they cast him into the den of lions, "Thy God whom whou servest continually, He will deliver thee." God did send His angel who delivered Daniel out of the lions' mouth. They also talked about how He delivered the three Hebrews out of the fiery furnace.

While they thus praised God for sending His angel to encamp about them to guard them continually, and especially for deliverance during this night of extreme danger, it seemed to them as though the room was filled with the glory of the Lord and one wave of unspeakable joy after another swept over them and flooded their souls.

The next morning a young man who was working in the ore mines not far from the place of the robbery said to some of the workmen, "Did you hear already that robbers had broken into the house of ———?" This young man was the first one to publish the incident as the old people had not yet told any of the neighbors anything about what had happened. He was at once regarded with suspicion, arousing the whole neighborhood with indignation as these aged people were held in high esteem by all those who knew them. Many of the neighbors advised them to employ detectives to try and arrest the burglar if possible. They, however, thought they did not care to go to law about the matter, being thankful that God had so gloriously delivered them. So the neighbors took the matter in hand, notified the county detective who had the burglar behind the bars in a short time.

One night, about two weeks before the time set for the trial, Grandfather had a very significant dream which caused him to awake. He awoke Grandmother and as he was telling her this dream, they heard a noise downstairs. They arose and went down and found that another robber had been in the house. They searched all around and found that he had stolen some provisions and a little money. They also noticed that he had left the coffee box, which was about half full of ground coffee, standing on the table uncovered.

They had been told that the father of the man in jail had made the remark to someone in the neighborhood a few days before, that "These people are old and might die yet before the trial, what will happen then? Can the matter be pushed further yet?" In view of this, and the dream Grandfather had that night, they were suspicious and had the coffee examined and found that the man who broke in that night had put poison into the coffee to poison them.

So then, the second time, God had marvelously protected them from the hands of would be murderers.

Several years after this incident, Grandmother fell asleep in Jesus and was laid to rest in the quiet country churchyard back of the old brick church.

Grandfather, though bereft of his earthly companion in the tests and trials of life, continued for many years in the service of the Lord. We were often refreshed when we heard him relate the above remarkable miracles of God's protection and care, while his eyes were filled with tears of joy and gratitude and his soul so full of glory that he could hardly speak. These things were always remarkably clear and fresh in his memory.

He lived to within a few years of the century mark, well in body, clear in mind, strong in faith, conscious of God's presence with him unto the end, when worn out and full of days though without sickness and pain he also fell asleep in Jesus and was carried to his last resting place by the side of his companion.

Here is another proof of the truthfulness of the Scriptures — "The angel of the Lord encampeth round about them that fear Him and delivereth them," and again, "Godliness is profitable unto all things, having promise of the life that now is, and of that which is to come."

NOTE: The above narrative first appeared in the Gospel Herald, March 22, 1913. This weekly was edited and published for thirty-two years, until his death in 1938, by W. B. Musselman, a grandson of David. At this printing, fall of 1972, there are two David Musselmans, great, great, great grandsons of the subject of this story, who are singing and playing musical instruments for the Lord, in many states. They are 21 and 22 years old. They are second cousins. One David sings and plays the piano on The Old Time Gospel Hour T.V. program from Lynchburg, Va. The other David travels from his base of Youngstown, Ohio, with five other young men in a large private bus, singing the Gospel full time in churches, large and small, in schools, clubs, fairs, etc.

C.H.B.

Living Poem
by Eusebius Hershey

It would take a book to tell the whole story of this man. In brief, he is a mystery, a marvel, a man of steel, a man of God, a preacher and a missionary. He was one of the early guiding spirits of our church. Truly he was an unsung hero, for few people know of him or the impact he made. He left his home and family to travel to the wilderness of Kansas and Missouri and made numerous trips to Canada on foot and horseback, ministering all the while.

At sixty-seven Eusebius left his wife and family to go to Liberia, Africa, as a missionary. This obedience to God's call cost him his life but earned him the privilege of being considered the first known missionary of the North American Mennonite bodies.

Hershey was built of the rough and tough stuff that made pioneers, but he was also gentle and tender enough to write poetry. Imagine this man writing one hundred verses for his fiftieth birthday!

Eusebius Hershey, born August 14, 1823 - died May 24, 1891, was truly one of God's chosen men.

The following verses are taken from his book *The Living Poem*, Second edition, 1878. The verses of "Introduction" and "50th Birthday" tell about Hershey, The Man. The "Centennial Hymn" provides insight into our country at the time of its one hundredth birthday. "Sketches in Poetry" is a sample of the message the Evangelist preached. A father's tender concern for his family is reflected in "A Father's Letter To His Married Daughter." Now go with the man, on foot and horseback. Share his experiences, his joys and sorrows in the "Distance of Miles" and the touching "10th Visit to Ontario."

Editor

Living Poem

A work for God in poetry!
The Author's name outside you'll see;
The seals are broken, read it through—
Let prejudice not hinder you.

Whether a saint or sinner yet,
This book will speak when he is dead:
May precious souls be snatched from hell,
And I with such in glory dwell.

Introduction

God gave to us a holy book,
My eyes in it did often look;
A little stream from it may run
To honor Him, the Triune One.

God's book is the best book of all,
It shows to man how deep his fall,
And tells him how to rise again,
By living faith in Jesus' name.

When I was young God's book I read;
I learned that I in sin was dead:
To thousands, now I wish to say,
How I found Christ, the Living Way.

A little book may come in print,
Readers may find therein plain hint;
To saints and sinners speaking straight,
Of a narrow way with the straight gate.

My Introduction shows above,
God and His book I first must love.
My name and birth-day I will give,
My parents' names, where we did live.

I'll rhyme it all, from first to last,
The present, future and the past;
God's help I need, He is my guide,
In His firm promise I'll confide.

My parent's names without fancy,
Hershey, Abraham and Nancy;
God to them nine children gave,
Two, like them, found each a grave.

My birth-day came, as all may see,
In eighteen hundred and twenty-three;
August, on the fourteenth day:
Since, millions died and passed away.

The place where we for years did live,
I'll to the reader plainly give:
Lancaster County, and Pa.,
Three miles of Manheim, north, I say.

While I now on my knees do write,
That once dear home is out of sight:
By faith I see that heavenly home,
Where death and sorrow ne'er can come,

I'm now in my fifty-fourth year,
This year, in print, it may appear,

The book that I for God shall give,
If I in health some months shall live.

With opposition I may meet,
If so, that makes the bitter sweet.
If I am led by God's strong hand,
This book may reach some distant land.

My Introduction may seem queer
When it to thousands doth appear:
Let prejudice not hinder you,
Read all the rhymes, till you are through.

And when God's spirit seals the truth,
Whether old in years, middle-aged or youth,
Then treasure up the good you'll find.
Love God, the Maker of mankind.

My given name the book will tell,
If some can't read it, try and spell;
It stands in rhymes, as you may see:
When you read it, remember me.

I speak to kings and princes too,
To high and low, what each should do
To honor Him, who reigns on high;
All mortals soon in dust must lie.

All who love here the King of kings.
Willing despise all trifling things;
All such shall live with Christ on high,
Where the redeemed shall never die.

For this the Saviour bled and died,
So shamefully was crucified;
Now, "It is finished," Christ did say,
"He is the Life, the Truth, the Way."

Let all the world before God bow.
Accept in Christ salvation now,
And glorify Him while below,
Then such may safe to heaven go.

In heaven such will not sorry be,
Who often here did bow the knee,
Denied themselves, and bore their cross,
And counted all things here but dross.

Some hundred verses I did write,
Some by day, and some by night,
If God will help I'll link them in,
I wish indeed to do no sin.

The reader then will clearly see,
How God in providence led me:

On different subjects I did write,
I did it humbly with delight.

Some trifling one perhaps will laugh,
And say the matter is all chaff;
Common people wheat will find,
Instruction for the honest mind.

Jesus Christ was perfect here,
To some he did quite mad appear;
"He hath a devil," some did say,
Such would not walk this narrow way.

Strange if all would praise this book,
Such who read and in it look.
Millions the Bible do despise,
By doing so, thing they are wise.

If I reach heaven, that happy place,
With millions see my Saviour's face;
I'll praise with them, the Triune One,
The Father, Spirit and the Son.

Fiftieth Birth-Day

On my fiftieth birth-day I will write
Thoughts which are beyond my sight.
As God directs so will I do,
I have His glory now in view!

August, this, the fourteenth day,
Eighteen seventy-three, I say.
This day to me is more than naught;
I know that I from God am taught.

In future days some one may see
What God, my Saviour, did for me;
Sinners may come, give God the heart,
Weak saints may make for heaven fresh start.

Impresion on my mind God made,
That I should write before too late:
I am not schooled so well in letter,
In Grammar some may do it better.

My thoughts run back to years when young,
When I was not in body strong;
God's spirit with my heart did strive,
At ten I lived no pious life.

I went from Jesus far away
In wickedness and idle play.
God called me oft by day and night,
To live in sin was my delight.

His goodness I so oft abused;
His holy name I did misuse.
On the broad road to hell I went,
I thought in future I'll repent.

Satan promised to me long life.
When I was married, had a wife,
I then could leave the way of sin—
A godly life might then begin.

I learned that Satan was a liar—
God's ways and thoughts indeed are higher.
Satan points to things below,
The pilgrim still must upward go.

When I was eighteen years of age,
I then took sick, I was not safe;
The fever made my body weak.
For help I did the doctor seek.

His medicine I then did take
But that did not the fever break.
The many sins I did commit
I found them now against me writ.

Both soul and body now felt sick,
Something I must do, yes, do it quick:
My soul was filled with guilty fears,
I sought the Lord in prayer with tears.

On my knees, I cried, Lord, save;
Sin had brought me near my grave;
My friends did give to me good-by,
They though I would soon in death cold lie.

Next door to death I knew I laid,
My sorrow now was very great;
I felt God's spirit drawing nigh,
In mercy He did hear my cry.

A burden from my heart did roll—
I felt Christ precious to my soul.
My soul and body He made well,
He snatched me as a brand from hell.

The first I then indeed did do,
I praised the Lord, my song was new:
Of Jesus' name I then did sing,
He is my Prophet, Priest, and King.

The next I then with tongue did say,
I said to friends, Fall down and pray,
Pray God that he your sins forgive,
You also may in Jesus live.

My father, up to fifty old,
He said his heart in sin was cold,
He could not pray, he said to me,
I said, Father, pray, God still loves thee.

That night I hope I'll ne'er forget,
It lives still in my memory yet;
That night, my soul was born again,
God's love doth yet with me remain.

More worth to me than glittering wealth,
Yes, food, or clothes, or even health,
Cannot to me such blessings give,
As I in Jesus do receive.

Fifty years, this day, I'm old,
In death, my hand may soon be cold.
This day to me is very dear,
With filial love my God I fear.

I know not where my pen shall stop,
The ink is willing still to drop,
While God still gives to my weak heart,
From writing I will not depart.

Useful language God may give
To such who would for Jesus live.
Some precious soul who went astray,
Instruction here may find, some day.

When God through grace my heart did change,
My young companions thought it strange
That I no more with them would go
The road that leads to endless woe.

They lived in sin, and I in grace,
I found true joy in wisdom's ways;
They thought indeed it could not be
That I with them they could not see.

They knew not I a way had found
Which leads to that celestial ground:
I said to them now come and see
Give God your heart and go with me.

Some came and cried, Have mercy, Lord,
According to thy holy word.
Many sought and found indeed
Sin is bitter, grace more sweet.

Of that number, some have gone,
Soon their pilgrimage did run;
Such who loved God to their end,
Now in heaven will not repent.

Some have acted like the dumb dog,
No more the ways of God would walk,
Vomited and like swine in mire,
Have turned for everlasting fire.

The devil often tempted me
To sin, that I sould wretched be;
Sometimes he almost gained the day,
To lead me from the heavenly way.

I would not for all this vain world
Give Jesus and to hell be hurled;—
Jesus is worth to me, yes, more
Than all this world with all its store.

For soon this world will pass away
By fire, says God, in that great day.
True riches, pilgrims, there shall find,
Because they left this world behind.

Perhaps some one would like to know
How God did lead me here below,
After he had pardoned me
Some stranger now would like to see.

When God had raised me from my bed
Thousand points I might give yet,
Whatever God will give to me
Then you may read and wonders see.

Eighteen years, I then was old,
The grace of God did make me bold,
God moved my heart and said I must
Speak to souls in Him should trust.

Illiterate I a boy was then,
I had to speak to some learned men.
With trembling heart, I oft did speak,
My teacher, Jesus, He was meek.

I should not mind what such would say,
Who would despise this humble way;
That I should speak what God would give,
Some will reject, some will believe.

Some years I preached not far from home—
I knew that I was not alone,
My Jesus still stood to my side,
In His firm promise could I confide.

My earthly father I did respect,
I was then a young man yet.
For him I worked on farm and mill,
I honored him and pleased him still.

My heavenly Father spoke to me,
So loud that I could hear and see,
He said that He had work from home,
When I at home my work had done.

One day I spoke, with tears in eyes,
To my earthly father, here's no lies,
My heavenly Father hath work for me
Far from home, I'll tell it thee.

He said he would not hinder me,
To go he said I should be free.
My Saviour's call I should obey;
He wished me luck, as he would say.

Father and sister I gave good-by,
My mother, in her grave did lie:
The state Ohio, was the ground
Where I appointed work have found.

'Tis there I went from east to west,
From south to north as God thought best,
He gave me work by day and night,
To do his will was my delight.

In twenty-nine counties traveled through,
I always found some work to do,
Many points I must omit,
I might bring in and make them fit.

My object was to glorify
The God who reigns above the sky;
That object I have still in view,
In all I think, or say, or do.

When I came back, I found all well,
To father and sisters I could tell,
How kind the Lord had been to me,
We once more could each other see,

But long at home I could not rest,
God moved my heart still further west:
Next year I went to Iowa,
God showed me how long there to stay.

On the land and on the deep,
Jesus told me still to speak,
Some would laugh and others weep,
My Jesus I would near me keep.

When I my work that year had done,
I started eastward, reached safe home;
Found my friends, as usual, well;
But long with them I could not dwell.

I helped my father build a barn,
It was a favor, and no harm;
My conscience I would still keep clear,
In heavenly love and godly fear.

The time again did now draw nigh,
That I to friends must say, good-by;
To western soil again must go,
There the Gospel trump to blow.

In my father's house we met,
We had a solemn meeting, yet;
Next day we parted through grace;
Since, never saw my father's face.

I left again, for west was bound;
But went first east, then north, around
I traveled both by land and sea,
My Saviour still was kind to me.

Thus I traveled far and wide,
And preached the word by day and night.
Solemn news my ears did meet,
Which caused mine eyes soon tears to weep.

My earthly father is no more,
The letter said, he left this shore;
Thousands of times I prayed for him,
I hope the Lord forgave his sin,

I hope to God his soul is safe.
When I came back I saw his grave,
But could not talk as heretofore,
Because I heard his voice no more.

Eight sisters, I had not another,
I, the ninth, their only brother;
Seven of them were each a wife,
I and the youngest single life.

The youngest, too, was married, then
Some years I staid as single men,
God led me still in his own way,
To preach the word by night and day.

Thus I was led from day to day,
In my Lord's appointed way,
I wished to live a pious life,
And trusted God for a house-wife.

God gave me one, 'twas Mary Ann,
I'll give some points, while yet I can;
My age was near twenty-eight years,
We married in God's holy fears.

She counted years two more than I,
But who can tell, which first must die;
Twenty-two years since we have met,
To-day, we are together yet.

The Lord to us one heir did give,
Twenty-one years with us did live,
The twenty-second, she began—
Nancy took for life a man.

Since I did change my single state,
God's love to us has been so great,
I realized His promised grace,
Since I have found His smiling face.

My heart this day doth thank the Lord,
For all the promise in His word,
Millions did so sudden die,
Thousands on sick beds do lie.

Denying grace with Him is found.
When I left home His word to sound,
Six times I went to British soil,
For souls there I would work and toil.

Some one might think I'm boasting here,
No, I write now in my God's fear:
Of God's grace alone I boast,
I care not for a wicked host.

The fiftieth birth-day, 'tis for me,
This day I never more shall see:—
This day, indeed, may be my last—
I write of things which are now past.

Some may think the man is weak,
Others say 'tis self he seeks;
The question is, what God will say,
I know I'm in the good old way.

A little more I ought to write,
Of my labor day and night,
How God did lead in seventy-two,
His mercies to us were not few.

The Lord had put it in my mind,
To leave my family behind;
To Western States once more to go;
The gospel trumpet there to blow.

I left my home the first of May,
God had been with me night and day;
And by His strong and mighty hand,
Has led me safe on Kansas land.

Some months, for God, I there did spead
On Kansas soil; I'll not repent
That I went forth as God did lead:
I felt His love divinely sweet.

'Twas there I stood on heathen ground,
The Indians heard the gospel sound,
By me and friend, who wished them well,
We taught them how in God to dwell.

They need, indeed, the Christian's love,
To teach them of those things above;
And tell them how to live below,
If we would safe to heaven go.

When I left home I traveled west;
I then turned north, I thought it best
To travel forth as God would lead:
Sinners daily I would meet.

To them I said, Oh, stop and think,
Oh, do not sport upon the brink!
But do now, while you may, return,
Or else you must foreve burn.

Some self-denial I passed through,
I give not many, but a few:
Through the streams I had to wade,
Bridges there were rarely made.

I traveled through cold, sometimes in heat,
God's approbation wished to meet:
I never felt right satisfied,
Unless I had God glorified.

One night I was locked in a room,
Thank God, I was not there alone,
I had my Saviour with me there,
Could praise His name, and say my prayer.

Next morning, thank God, I came out,
My soul felt happy, I could shout:
I then proceeded on my journey
In good humor, with my pony.

The robbers took from me my money,—
The love of God, more sweet than honey,
They could not take that from my heart,
My Saviour would not from me part.

Thus I went forth from day to day,
In my Lord's appointed way;
Not knowing where a home I'd find,
Some are stingy, some are kind.

I spoke for Jesus in each State,
Sometimes early, sometimes late;
On streets, in houses, souls did hear
Of that God whom all should fear.

When I reached home and found all safe,
And none had gone to the cold grave,
It did indeed me so much please,
I thanked the Lord upon my knees.

Five months and eighteen days I spent,
In love for souls I'll not repent.
I promised God for Him to live
While He me life and grace shall give.

Near ten months have now run round
Since I returned from Kansas ground;
I preached here in my native State,
To high and low, to rich and great.

To-day I'm fifty years of age,
I may be very near my grave;
I say the will of God be done,
I know I'm on my journey home.

Before I die I think to go,
The seventh time to Ontario.
Good seed to sow on British soil,
For my Saviour, work and toil.

How soon the hour of death will come
To call us hence to our long home!
God alone, he knows, can tell,
May none of us go down to hell.

I, my daughter, and my wife,
To-day thank God we are alive,
My son-in-law comes in as four,
My mother-in-law her two sons more.

Next week the number may decrease,
Four may stay and three may leave.
If we shall take the parting hand,
Perhaps never to meet here in this land.

If this indeed should happen so
That we could never meet below,
May we then meet in heaven above,
Where all is peace and all is love.

The shade of night now falls on me,
To write I soon no more can see;
The night of death—it soon will come,
May I then have my work well done.

I'll now wind up my poet lines,
Perhaps some more in future rhymes
If God leads me some more may write,
Some by day and some by night.

My name I now will give below
Each line a letter is to show
The name of him, his fiftieth year,
One hundred verses seem quite queer.

Eternal are thy mercies, Lord,
Union Spirit, Word and God;
Saviour and God, in spirit one,
Emmanuel said, God's will be done,.

Be this my daily language, Lord;
Inspire my soul, thou Living Word;
Unite me steadfastly to God,
Safe path which all the pious trod.

Heaven on earth begins within:
Eternal joy's more sweet than sin.
Rest for the weary spirit here;
Such as serve God with filial fear.

Come Father, Son, and Holy Ghost,
Help me with all the heavenly host,
Eternal hallelujahs sing;
Yes, there my praise more perfect bring.

Centennial Hymn

United States of America:
Centennial, hundred years, they say.
The God who other nations knew,
Saw what United States would do.

One hundred years we say are past,
Since Declaration's news went fast
From North to South, from East to West;
The act was done they though the best.

Those hands which wrote in a great haste,
They hoped they did not paper waste;
They wished that those who followed them
Might honest be, true godly men.

Millions have died, we know, since then,
Not all of whom were honest men;
If Washington could now come back,
He'd find that many things still lack.

A hundred years! What is the best?
Thanks be to God! the slaves found rest.

67

Their shackles broke and they are free,
Many, such things, don't like to see.

Dear colored race, we wish you well;
Christ died to save a world from hell:
Let all who are yet bound in sin
To Jesus come, He'll take them in.

In our blessed United States
Many a one his brother hates;
Democrats think that they are down;
Republicans shan't wear the crown.

What is the name, the party name?
The name is after all the same.
The thing is this—Which does the right?
God in that people doth delight.

God, who does the nations rule,
Wants good men, employs no fool;
In wisdom He His will performs,
In sunshine, and sometimes by storms.

Philadelphia—Brotherly love!
God, who also rules above,
Has fixed His eyes on that great spot,
Where Red Men long ago have trod.

They worshiped the Great Spirit there
In ignorance, with honest prayer.
Why do those kings and princes meet?
Is it to worship at God's feet?

President and Governors too,
Meet there now, but what to do?
WIth other men in office high,
Is it their God to glorify?

God looks for this: ye great men hear;
Great wisdom did to us appear;
Then as a nation, we should be
Thankful to God for all we see.

Centennial now, one hundred years;
Some years ago there were some fears,
That our blessed land would ruined be;
Many then wished that day to see.

Thanks be to God the Union stands!
But who can tell when breaks the bands?
We are in danger surely so,
Hear it all, both high and low.

All the slaves are not yet free;
Many in the North we see.

Intemperance, pride, and what else more,
Tie millions on our blessed shore.

Let watchmen all on Zion's wall,
Be faithful to their heavenly call;
And live as watchmen ought to live,
Their people all fair warning give.

I think if this would soon take place,
We may look out for better days;
The President and Congress too,
With all in office justly do.

A happy nation we have been,
God, of course, much sin has seen;
Yet, if we all amend our ways,
Then we shall soon see better days.

Union between God and the soul,
In families love the hearts control;
Churches and nations catch the flame,
Might soon be one in Jesus' name.

Then no more say Centennial year,
The great Millennium would appear;
Philadelphia then would be too small,
For us to see God's wonders all.

God hath a place prepared for that,
Those eyes that see it shall be glad;
Wonders which earth could never show,
After Gabriel did the trumpet blow.

Then Jesus reigns from shore to shore:
Then sin and strife will be no more;
The cannon's roar shall silenced be,
All nations then in Christ agree.

Don't open the Sabbath-day,
That show of natural things, I say,
Let God and all the nations know
That we are more than brutes below.

Let Jesus and his blessed word
By foreighn nations here be hears.
When they return, then they can say,
America keeps the Sabbath-day.

If we transgress this great command,
Profane the Sabbath in our land;
God's judgment he'll to us reveal,
If we the Sabbath-day will steal.

I gave my thoughts in words quite brief;
God gave them to me, I believe,

To leave in print—to edify—
For high and low before they die.

May God bless it to thousands yet,
My hand which wrote will soon be dead.
My object is to glorify
The God who reigns above the sky.

Examine it impartial through,
And when you find some work to do,
Don't wait awhile but now begin,
Be sure to cease from every sin.

All earthly kindgoms soon will fall,
When Jesus willb be all in all;
Then he shall reign, yes, he alone,
High on his everlasting throne.

EUSEBIUS HERSHEY is my name,
I seek not here for earthly fame.
Rebersburg is my address,
In Christ I seek my happiness.

Centre County now comes in,
I know I hate the ways of sin.
Pennsylvania comes below,
From earth to heaven I hope to go.

Sketches In Poetry

Readers now would like to know,
What texts I generally had, that's so,
God helps to give some now to thee,
Into God's book I'll point, then see.

The first I took, was Matthew five,
The eighth verse, look out for life:
The heart that beats by day and night,
Sinners in God find no delight.

Their hearts are impure, filled with sin,
Evil spirits dwell within.
If sinners pray, God cleanse my heart,
Unclean spirits then must depart.

The love of God then fills the soul,
Satan doth not now hold control;
Jesus now doth reign within,
The blood of Christ doth cleanse from sin,

Blessed are such, Christ did say so,
While they the narrow way do go;
They see God. Oh, wondrous sight!
Such worship him with pure delight.

Now such must show by word and deed,
That they are changed in heart, that's sweet.
The pure in heart will show good fruit,
A spiritual life is their pursuit.

If such till death shall faithful be,
In heaven they shall their Father see
But sinners must from Christ depart
Who in death have no pure heart.

The substance of my sermons were
A change of heart, then honest prayer;
To God and man must be sincere
If we would safe in Heaven appear.

From Genesis to Malachi,
Good texts I found, I'll tell thee why,
I found all through the Golden Chain,
In proper time the Saviour came.

From Matthew, Mark, Luke, and St. John.
Hark what I say, I'm not yet done.
The Epistles, Acts, Revelations, too,
I found good texts, yes, not a few.

The other text I now shall give,
Thankful, I hope, some will receive
The text and substance with the place:
I spoke for God, He gave me grace.

The book of Job there you can read
The 14th chapter, when you meet
The 14th verse, then stop and think
Of him who speaks with pen and ink.

In Ohio I that text did seek,
God helped me to His glory speak:
I was requested so to do,
The man's name I might give, too.

I'll make it brief for fear some might
Think the man is puffed with pride.
All I have God gave to me,
Why should I then so foolish be?

The Scriptures tells us man doth die,
The God who lives and reigns on high,
Declared if man will disobey
He then shall die and pass away.

Now death doth reign in every land,
It breaks the matrimonial band;
When death doth come the soul must go
To heaven, or sink to endless woe.

When Christ shall come the second time,
The dead shall rise in every clime;
The saints have bodies glorified,
And with their spirit did unite.

All sinners for damnation rise,
They acted foolish were not wise.
Christ, the Saviour, did teach so,
Eternal life and endless woe.

For proof do in the Bible look,
The Gift of God, O blessed Book;
In it we read of heaven and hell,
In one of these the dead shall dwell.

What doth the Infidel here say,
If man shall die and pass away;
He and the beast lie on one heap,
In death they shall forever sleep.

The Spiritualist doth not say so,
Adam's God placed man here below.
Those who die in sin, they say
Find heaven in working their own way.

The Universalist then next comes in,
And says if any die in sin,
The new birth they don't need at all,
Christ tasteth death, they say, for all.

The Christian says a different thing,
He did repent and now hates sin;
Through grace he strives for holiness,
In Christ he finds true happiness.

The Skeptic now deep in the mire
Of unbelief, he scorns hell fire,
The Christian stands firm on his rock,
No skeptic lies can make him shock.

The heathen Indian feels quite lonely,
When a brother dies he kills a pony;
The pole now with the bridle raise,
And brings his food to last three days.

In three days, he thinks the pony run,
Where Indians live and use the gun:
He leaves the brother there to fish,
To hunt and sport—this is their wish.

Let sinners all before God bow,
Accept the blessed Saviour now,
Repent, believe, give God your heart,
And from your selfish way depart.

If so you do you'll find a Friend,
On whom you can for help depend;
When death shall close your mortal eyes,
You'll live with Christ, beyond the skies.

Oh, what a joy! Oh, what a bliss!
If we shall meet where Jesus is.
Sorrow and death shall be no more,
When we have reached that heavenly shore.

Then with the blessed and heavenly host,
Praise Father, Son and Holy Ghost;
And live with Christ for evermore,
And sing at home to die no more.

A Father's Letter to His Married Daughter

A parent's likeness in this letter;
Some give show, I think 'tis better
Sound counsel to our children give,
And holy conduct while we live.

Here in the room where you did sleep,
With solemn thoughts and feelings deep,
To you I write, upon my knees;
A father's blessing,—love and peace.

Jacob and Nancy this is true,
These lines I send in love to you:
God strengthens me in mind and hand,
To write to a united band.

Deep interest in you both I feel,
Which I would thus to you reveal,
I love my Saviour here below,
But feel my weakness, God doth know.

In matrimony you are joined,
I know that God to us is kind,
Let Jesus Christ dwell in each heart,
And gladly from all sin depart.

If so you do, you'll find a Friend,
On whom you can for help depend,
In life and death, and in that day
When heaven and earth shall pass away.

Our prayers to God shall contant be,
While we each other's face can't see;
By night and day we think of you,
Be to each other always true.

When we were yet in number six,
And sang God's praise, our voice did mix,

That numbers less we now perceive,
Nancy did us this morning leave.

Your father thinks of years now past,
Perhaps this morning was the last,
That we on earth your faces see,
If I die soon, remember me.

The little stand where leans my head,
Is wet with tears that I have shed,
May many more God give to me,
To shed for you in sympathy.

Your welfare lies so near my heart,
How hard it seems that we must part;
How can my heart so soon get cold
Against the child that left our fold.

The nineteenth day of August, now,
This morning, we before God bow;
After reading from God's Word,
Then by prayer approach the Lord.

And when, as usual, we do sing,
The praise of our Eternal King,
Our voices now in number, two;
And as we sing we think of you.

The day is past, the night has come,
I'm at the desk in the front room,
My Saviour hath still kept in store,
Helps me to give a few lines more.

To-morrow if the Lord says so,
I'll start for British Ontario,
I'll visit first the Buckeye State,
Then from Cleveland, cross the lake.

While I am yet alive and well,
I'll go and the blest story tell,
How Jesus died for all mankind,
Oh, may not one be left behind!

My object is to glorify
God while I live before I die,
I'll speak, sing, pray, and letters write:
To do God's will is my delight.

I now do say to you, Good-night,
If I shall live till morning light,
What God will give that will I write
To you while you are out of sight.

'Tis August now, the twentieth day,
The time is passing fast away;

God kept us safe throughout the night,
In family worship we unite.

Mother is willing I should send
Some lines from her: Oh, to repent!
Give God your hearts without delay,
Oh! Think of that great judgment day.

Perhaps we'll meet on earth no more,
We hope then on that heavenly shore.
Oh, yes! to meet in that blessed land,
And no more take the parting hand.

Farewell Jacob, and Nancy, too,
Be always to each other true:
Eusebius Hershey and my wife,
Dear children live a pious life.

My address I to you now give,
To write while we and you shall live,
For though we may be far apart,
Undying love should fill each heart.

EUSEBIUS HERSHEY is my name,
I seek not here for earthly fame.
Rebersburg is my address,
In Christ I seek my happiness.

Centre County now comes in,
I know I hate the ways of sin.
Pennsylvania comes below,
From earth to heaven I hope to go.

Distance of Miles

In Pennsylvania, also in Iowa,
Many hundred miles did walk, I say,
In Kansas and on British soil,
Walked many miles, for Christ did toil.

Over the Alleghanies went
On foot, for God, I'll not repent;
Over these mountains I could walk,
Young then, but did for Jesus talk.

Thousands of miles on different lakes,
On rivers too, in different States,
On railroads, God knows best, how far
On horseback, wagon, some grease was tar.

How many thousands it would count
In miles, the way I went around;
One million may be most too high,
I'll leave the figure with God lie.

To young preachers I would say,
If you are called by God, you may
Deny yourself, as Christ did do,
And His example may pursue.

But you must watch as well as pray,
Satan has snares along the way,
If you will play like trifling boys,
Satan will catch you with those toys.

You may not live as long as I,
Myself I know, I must soon die.
The people to which we do speak,
Should see we're both humble and meek.

The miles you travel may not be many,
Seek not for human praise or penny;
But seek in all your God to please,
Your usefulness with thus increase.

The Tenth Visit To Ontario

O God, I know Thy love to us is great.
In eighteen hundred and seventy-eight,
The month of March, now the sixth day,
I'll honor Thee while yet I may.

On British soil the tenth time, now
In writing I before God bow,
In Chief Henry's house I write
To God's glory with delight.

The second edition I must give
For others' welfare while I live;
Millions may read when I am dead,
When my hand rests in the cold bed.

Since I came here, to Indians dear,
What did before my eyes appear?
A tombstone—there I language found
Which said, one more is in the ground.

But who was he whose name I read?
Who now doth sleep among the dead?
My interpreter, Jones, Henry, dear,
His lovely voice I no more hear.

At his grave I low did bow,
To God I did renew my vow,
That I to Him would faithful be,
While His hand is leading me.

O Henry, I remember well,
When I and you God's truth did tell;

The Indians who did hear us speak,
Tears from their eyes did freely leak.

I hope the seed which we did sow,
Will richly to God's glory grow,
And multiply an hundred fold;
May thousands yet for Christ speak bold.

On the tombstone I did read,
Language to me dear and sweet;
I'll give it for my fellow-men,
Thus speak for God while yet I can.

The first I'll give: above did see,
The Book which points to Calvary
The emblem of that blessed Book;
My eyes delight in it to look.

The next, I saw, in memory dear,
Henry Jones did disappear,
March the first, in seventy-six,
God thirty-nine years his age did fix.

One verse I'll soon quite clearly give,
To benefit those who still do live;
They are indeed quite dear to me,
I'll give them now, let thousands see.

O sacred Grave, what precious dust
Is here committed to thy trust.
But, oh! the soul is fled on high,
To live with Christ, no more to die.

A tombstone like this I can kiss,
And think of that immortal bliss,
And think of those we loved so well,
And sing such joy no tongue can tell.

Guide me, O God, to write for Thee,
Yes, honest truth in poetry;
Inspire my heart, direct my pen,
Then let read the best learned men.

The sun shines warm to-day, indeed
I'm glad I with the Chief could meet,
In his house, at home, this day,
Here I can write, yes, read and pray.

Some readers may find fault with me,
When their eyes these lines do see;
If one in four is edified,
Then surely God is glorified.

This is the way good seed is sown,
The fourth part hath distinctly grown;

So Christ did say to mortal man,
I'll do for him the best I can.

If God will spare my life indeed,
Next Sabbath I'll the Indians meet;
By proxy, I intend to speak
Of Jesus, who was always meek.

My first interpreter is dead.
I hope there is a good man yet,
That I can use for God to speak.
My fellow-men's welfare I do seek.

Oh, may this still my object be,
To point all men to Calvary,
To sinners, may I earnest say,
Oh, turn to God while yet you may.

If you will come, give God your heart,
And from your sinful ways depart;
God hath promised you shall live,
Jesus will all your guilt forgive.

To saints I say, love Christ indeed,
And if you do with trials meet,
Then put your trust in Christ and pray,
Be faithful in the narrow way.

May all around you clearly see
That you remember Calvary;
And walk as children of the day,
With great delight that heavenly way.

My first edition came to print,
The paper good with lasting ink,
The year was "eighteen seventy-seven,"
God helped me by His grace from heaven.

The year which now is seventy-eight,
I hope the Book will have more weight:
Oh, may Instruction's light increase,
And may these lines true Pilgrims greet.

I'll not forget to give some lines,
God help to shape them in plain rhymes,
What happened to my pony, dear,
His life he lost so very queer.

In September, day twenty-eight,
In the evening, middling late,
D. Long's barn in Hartliton,
All on fire in flame did burn.

With fearful shrieks the beast did call,
When the great pain on him did fall;

Human ears did hear him cry,
No one to help him could come nigh.

Through the flames the course did lead,
There a painful death did meet,
Thousands of miles he carried me,
A providential hand I see.

I now do walk on British soil,
For Jesus I came here to toil;
I'll bear my cross and follow him,
May he keep me to do no sin.

Whether with Indian or White Man,
May I still do the best I can;
Work for Christ while yet I may,
For soon will come my dying day.

Ye ministers of the Gospel, hear!
And when these lines to you appear,
Then ask your hearts if you are true,
While you profess God's work to do.

What doth that mean, a castaway?
Paul of himself doth clearly say,
To others we might preach quite well,
Ourselves indeed be cast to hell.

Oh, may such words our hearts awake,
And every thing that's bad forsake,
Still do what we to others say,
By walking in the narrow way.

I thank the Lord that I could write,
In the Chiefs' house, with great delight;
At their table with them eat,
Their love to me was very sweet.

With them I had a pleasant stay;
Before we parted we did pray:
I thanked them for their love to me,
In heaven I wish them all to see.

I promised on next Sabbath day,
That I would preach to them and pray;
To all the Indians who would meet,
I with the Bible them would greet.

The Sabbath morning now hath come,
Some more writing must be done;
I walked and came to the graveyard,
There I had work ere I could part.

At my interpreter's grave did kneel,
My heart indeed did solemn feel;

For Jesus I began to write,
While the sun was shining bright.

Six verses I did here put down,
May heaven's blessing each one crown,
And God's blessing follow them,
When they are read by different men.

The first I'll give distinct and clear,
The other five will soon appear;
Then treasure up when you read six,
Your heart on God do steadfast fix.

Here in this grave a dear one lies,
We hear no more his groans and sighs;
His body now in the cold grave,
I hope his soul in heaven is safe.

Who is the one of which I speak?
The brother who I found once meek,
Henry Jones, who spoke by me,
His grave and tombstone here I see.

While I now at his grave do write,
I think of him—now out of sight;
On bended knees now at his grave,
May I meet him where we are safe.

There, where we take no parting hand,
In that bright and heavenly land;
There, where all tears are wiped away,
We'll sing God's praise in endless day.

O Brother Henry! you were dear
To me, but you did disappear;
Your wife and children God will bless,
May they meet you in happiness.

Oh, what a joy! Oh, what a bliss!
When we shall meet where Jesus is,
And there with Christ for ever dwell,
Sing Jesus hath done all things well.

From here I then did start to walk
To the Church, where I did talk
To many Indians who had come;
They heard what Christ for us had done.

The minister in charge was there,
Brother Jacks, who closed by prayer;
We sang, I prayed, and then did read.
The interpreter, Cabbage, had his seat

Near to me, he spoke for me;
I'll give correct, then you can see

How we did work for God so nice.
This interpreting it goes twice.

I read my text, then he did read,
In the Ojibbeway—to Indians sweet;
We had a meeting very good,
God had provided wholesome food.

I felt the Spirit hovering round,
WHile the Gospel clear did sound.
When we closed I wished to stay
With the Indians, sing and pray.

We had to hasten to French Bay,
I promised there some good to say;
Five miles we went, where I did talk.
A number of Indians there did walk.

Here we had a solemn time,
Although far in this Northern clime;
God's Spirit surely here was nigh.
Without remark I can't pass by.

Towards heaven, up lifted hand,
Each one of the Indian band
Expressed their thanks to God that way,
And to me what they heard say.

Before I left each hand did shake,
Wished thereby true friendship make,
We sang, "The Parting die no more,"
When we shall meet on that blessed shore.

O heaven, O heaven, that happy place!
Where I shall see my Saviour's face,
And meet the pious on that shore,
Where death and sorrow are no more.

My soul forget all trifling things;
Come, Lord, give me the spirit wings,
To soar above the world's delight,
And take from earthly toys my flight.

Then, when I think and when I speak,
May show always that I am meet.
And never speak a murmuring word,
But always trust my faithful Lord.

This tenth time now on British ground,
While I the Gospel trump do sound,
May I be sure God is with me,
His hand, oh may I daily see.

When I shall leave and go on home,
May I my work have faithful done;

A conscience clear not me condemn,
Nor by God, nor yet by men.

This is the blessing I shall crave,
How strictly then should I behave;
By day and night live in God's fear,
And safe at last in heaven appear.

At that great day, with joyful heart,
When all unfaithful must depart,
May I my Saviour hear say, Come;
If true to God, Christ says well done.

Many, many years ago,
The Indian tribes had war, that's so,
The Mohawks with the Ojibbeways,
I'll give some rhymes of those dark days.

They had not heard the Gospel sound,
They lived in darkness all around;
A savage spirit them did rule,
They did fight ont in Christ's school.

But oh! now hear the blessed news,
God sent to them the heavenly truth;
They did receive the Prince of Peace,
Wars and strife with them now cease.

I saw the ground where blood did flow,
Where many an Indian fell quite low;
The Ojibbeways and Mohawks too,
Have now a peaceful work to do.

Now when they meet, they shake the hand,
And show they are a Christian band.
That cruel spirit now did part,
They show that they have peace in heart.

Lord, send Thy truth from shore to shore,
May cruel men be found no more,
May every nation, every tongue,
By them be heard a peaceful song.

The Prince of Peace will have it so,
That all should honor Him below;
Come to His school and learn His praise,
Then sound it forth in endless days.

I'll now put down the seventy-three,
In future days some eyes may see
How God my Father doth lead me,
Prepares me for eternity.

I now do give the seventy-four,
Six different tribes of Indians more,

After I was homeward bound,
The Lod led me on Indian ground.

Over three thousand there do live.
Very brief some points I'll give;
I to their council meeting went,
Of that course I'll not repent.

The chiefs were there, some twenty-five,
Some of them were old in life,
They gave me privilege to speak;
Thanks be to God, that we could meet.

This meeting to me was so dear,
I spoke to them in my God's fear,
The chiefs and all, attention gave,
And every one did well behave.

I told them how we should live here
If we would safe in heaven appear,
Love God supremely with delight,
And do to fellow-men what's right.

If so, then we would meet above,
Where all is peace and heavenly love.
There nations meet from every clime,
Who served the Lord in their short time.

Some live here as pagans yet,
In scriptural knowledge they are dead;
They offer to their god a dog,
He must be white, yes white as chalk.

Speeches then their priest do make,
They think God did their offering take,
Their conscience now feels satisfied,
They think their god is glorified.

It is now May, day twenty-five,
I reached safe home, found all alive;
My family were, as usual, well:
Thank God that I such news can tell.

I now will give the eighty-three,
If I in health more days shall see,
To God's honor I will live,
My time and all to Him I'll give.

It is now June, yes, the fourth day,
My calling I must still obey.
Our Conference met in Quakertown,
From home I came the last week down.

Our meeting closed; to-day I came
To Philadelphia. In Christ's name

My writing I must finish soon,
I did commence this afternoon.

Eighty-six verses this will make,
The clock struck nine, it is not late;
I'll finish now by candle-light,
On my kneess I hope it's right.

My first edition I did close,
THen did sleep in sweet repose;
In this city went to bed.
A wonder that I'm not yet dead.

A year and some days since are past,
Since I for God did write here last;
A wonder that again I came,
To finish here in Jesus' name.

The LIVING POEM speaks quite free,
Impartial readers clear can see,
That for their welfare I did write,
To work for God is my delight.

Yes, when my hand is cold and dead,
This book will speak to sinners yet,
And say to such, give God your heart,
Or else you must from Christ depart.

To saints it says, to God be true,
To mortals your whole duty do;
This secures your hope for heaven,
Such have indeed all sins forgiven.

My ears did hear the clock stike ten,
I think I soon must stop my pen,
And hope to meet in heaven there
Who read this book careful with prayer.

Here in this room, where I did write
The first conclusion with delight,
The month of May in seventy-seven,
In the night about eleven.

In Philadelphia, June, in '78,
The second edition with its weight,
I'll close and thus be satisfied,
May all who read be edified.

The three last pages now I'll give,
Perhaps the last while I shall live,
In poetry, with ink and pen,
For the welfare of my fellow-men.

Oh, may my Father guide my hand!
Give useful words for every land;
For soon such lines will come in print,
Gospel truth with honest hint.

In all the book, I did not say
Of outward ceremony's way.
Of baptism, which is the right mode,
One passage I will briefly quote:

In Matthew, hear the Saviour say,
The Triune mode right on the way.
Father, Son and Holy Ghost,
Millions do follow, what a host!

Down in the water Christ did go,
And an example us did show;
Millions since then have followed him,
The pious who confessed their sin.

In the night he was betrayed,
He for us all a pattern made:
And washing his disciples' feet,
Love and humility here meet.

With his hands he did break the bread,
True Christians to the world are dead.
And in Christ's name the bread hey eat,
Invisible be with such does meet.

Thus we in Christ example see,
He says himself, Now follow me
In meekness and humility,
If so, in heaven my face shall see.

If any one does wisdom lack,
Then pray to God; Oh, be not slack!
God to such will give free grace
To follow Christ in their short days.

All outward forms are all in vain,
If we are not here born again;
So Christ did say; it is all true;
He speaks to all, he speaks to you.

Now I must surely close my lines;
I gave so much in hones rhymes;
I hope God will the increase give,
May millions turn to God and live.

Let honest Christians pray for me,
Soon if their eyes these lines shall see;
In my weakness I'll still go on
Till I meet Jesus on his throne.

Amen; my Father, may it be
That we in heaven Thy face shall see,
And there with all the shining host,
Praise Father, Son and Holy Ghost. Amen.

Autobiography of
Jacob Moyer
Copied from his original handwriting

Jacob Moyer was born October 16, 1842 and died in 1914. His life story related the way of life in that era for one who openly claimed to be "born again". He and his family lived in the Hatfield-Harleysville, Pennsylvania area. He played an important part in the founding of the Harleysville Church. He was known as "Rose Jelly Jakie" because he specialized in selling Rose Jelly Salve.

Editor

Vernfield, Pennsylvania
February 28th, 1910

I thought I should write some of my life, and the Lord leading, my prayer is that it may be a blessing to some one else and the Lord may be glorified.

I was born October 16th, 1842. My mother died with I was five weeks old, then my grandparents took me. I was so poorly that everybody thought, "this baby will die." One time a woman came up to the room and said the baby is dead. When they came in it still lived. One time I went with the hired girl to the creek where she did our washing. When she was at work I fell into the creek. When she looked up and could not see me she ran along the water, then she saw a hand above the water. She pulled me out but I did breathe no more. Then she held me upside down, then the water came out and I could breathe again. Glory to God.

When I was eight years old I got diptheria. I got it so hard that through it I lost part of my hearing. My voice was also injured—and other parts. By nature I was very lively. I was very font of books but my hearing and only four month school did hinder me to get a good education. I did hear no sermon or prayer but I did know so much of the Bible which they taught me at home that I did know that I was a sinner; but of a personal exsperience I heard nothing. They exhorted me to behave well and do better but this was impossible for me. I know my grand mother had much trouble about me and prayed much. (I hope to meet her in glory). I was full of fun. My greatest joy was to make people laugh. That was my life. When about eighteen years I learned cigar-making—and of course also chewing and smoking. I thought it looks so big to smoke and chew and curse. But all this time I had great fear about the end of the world. I some times dreamed that the world was on fire, and in many other ways did the Spirit convict me.

At the age of 24 I whent with my brother Abraham to Canada. I did like it very good out there but I did more in gambling and drinking and dancing than ever before. Often half nights and whole Sundays did we play cards. But the good Spirit did not leave me. I had deep conviction that time. I sometimes did run on my way home from my gambling for fear sombody would kill me. But when at home and had shut the door I found that the trouble was in my heart, then I promised the Lord, sometimes on my knees, if He would let me live only this night I would do better, but the next day it was worse than ever for I did not know how to get saved. I never heard that we could receive the forgiving of our sins in this world, but I thought we must do better, give up the world and its pleasures and get baptised—then we would get saved when we die. But it would then be too late—glory to God I know better now.

Several times drunken men tried to kill me but the Lord kept me from all harm. In this way I lived about 3 years. About the year 1870 a revival broke out in the old Mennonite Church in Waterloo County, Canada. Bro. Daniel Wismer began to hold meetings in private houses and some of my young companions got saved. This surprised me for I did not know what it meant to get saved, but I lived in the hotell—but that last year before the revival I felt so broken down in body and had pain in the heart and felt so condemned of my sins that I often hardly dared to sleep for fear that I would die and wake up in hell.

At last I felt I should go and see those people who got saved and hear for my-self what they had to say. Then they told me how they came to Jesus as poor sinners and how the Lord had forgiven all their sins, and how happy they felt and did prais the Lord for his goodness and said with what joy they could now obey the Lord. Then I felt that this is just what I did need. I was often among them for a few month, then one night when they prayed to-gether the Holy Spirit got hold of me and from that time I was willing to seek the Lord but I was so ignorant and felt such a great sinner that I could not believe that such a big sinner could be saved. I did not know the difference between the old and the new thestament. They tried hard to help me through.

I lived still in the hotel and made cigars and nearly got back in my old life. When my dear brethren and sisters saw this they persuadet me to go with them to Port Elgin for a week—100 miles by team. The devil tried hard to keep me back but the Lord did help and I went with them—glory to God. Up there was a lively class. They prayed much with me for a few days but it seemed to me that my sins did reach to heaven. I felt as if everybody else could be saved but not myself. But one day Amos Bowman took me alone and read and spoke a good while with me. At last he said, "Jesus has taken away all sins." Then in a moment it went through my heart—if He has taken them all away mine must be too. Then the burden was gone, Glory to God. I had to lauph by myself for joy. For a few days I did hardly dare to believe it was true. The devil said it was not true—you are not saved, but I prayed to God to show me if I am right or not. Then in a moment I was so filled with the Spirit—and He gave witness to my spirit.

O I was so glad and went from house to house to tell the good news—Glory to God. I thought everybody would be glad to hear that Jesus forgave all my sins, but some got mad, but I was glad. When I came home the wife of my host said, it is not necessary to make such a fuss. She said I take my prayer Book and go alone it is enough when I pray that way, but years afterwards I had prayer-meeting in her Hotel; Praise the Lord O my Soul.

Next came my Business. I was a cigarmaker and was in partnership with an unconverted man. I asked our preacher if it were wrong for a Christian to make cigars. He said he did not know, I should ask the Lord, and so I did. The cause the Preacher could not tell me which was rite, he smoked himself that time. But he got light afterwards. Then I went to work. Then the Spirit began to show me that this work was not for me because it is enjourious to Health and much fraud was in the Business and nobody was profited by my work, and a christian should work for the good of his fellowmen. It was not easy for me to give up, but at last such fear came over me that I could stand it no longer. Then I went out of the shop and left it all to my partner to settle all. I never got anything out of it, but I was not sorry about it today. I am glad I left all for Jesus sake. He saved and cleansed also from smoking and chewing. He made me perfectly free from the filthy weed. Glory to his name.

After nearly 40 years, I am still happy on the way, praise his Holy name. My old companions in the hotel tried hard to get me to play cards or smoke or drink, but the Lord kept me firm. When they saw that they could do nothing, they said you are a fool and you will stay a fool. Glory to God that I ever became a fool for Christ's sake. Next came Public confession.

In the meetings the devil said you cannot speak in Public, you do not hear what the Brethren and Sisters say, then perhaps you'd say something that is not in place, then they will laugh at you. So he kept me still but, I had no rest. The Spirit did strive with me to get me to work, but the Devil tried just as hard to keep still. When others confessed and got Blessed I had nothing and was much troubled with doubts.

The devil said you are not saved, you do not feel like the others. So it went on for about a year, then by the help of God through Dear Bro. Noah Detwiler, I broke through. O it was blessed when I began to tell in Public what Jesus had done for me and it is yet my greatest joy, Halaluja. Some people think it is boasting to tell what the Lord has done for us, yet it is, but not of ourselves, but of the Lord as often as we sincerely from the heart tell what the Lord has done for us. We honor him and he Blessed us. Now about Baptism. I had some trouble. We had no church at the time and the one in which the revival began did Baptise by sprinkling, but I felt and told them I should be immersed but they did not allow it, so I thought when others could be satisfied with that perhaps I could too, but I could not. For 4 years I was troubled about it, then I got immersed—Glory to God. When I came out of the water, I saw the way open from earth to heaven. A few years after my conversion I felt I should do more for the Lord and the Salvation of others. This I thought I could not do to visit people and talk and pray with them. At last I got willing, but I got such hard opposition from cold proffessors that I gave it up again. They said, what would become of the people if all would go around and talk and pray. So the devil got the victory this time.

Afterwards I went to my old home in Pennsylvania for a year or so. There I did much visiting and the Lord Blessed me—Glory to His Name. When I came back to Canada the Lord shewed me that I should made my home at Sam Snyders and labor by the day for a living, and visit the people. But the devil said maybe you will not get much work, you better hire yourself this summer to Benji. Snyders, then you are sure to get your money, then you can go and work for the Lord. There I did know that it came from the devil and I obeyed him. Then the Lord put me under the rod for 3 months. I had such an up and down life that even Gods children did not know what to think of me. The more I prayed, the worse I got. At last it was unbearable, I did not know this 3 months what was the matter, but one morning in family prayer I could bear it no longer. I cried from the depth of my heart what is the cause and what shall I do. Then the Lord shoed me back 3 months where he wanted me to work for him and that this was the cause of my trouble. Then I got willing as never before to work for the Lord. Then the Devil said you have nothing when you get old and maybe you can get no home, but I said I will obey the Lord if I must carry my goods in a bundle on my back. Then I had the victory, and the Lord Blessed me wonderfully and I got the best home at Bro. Sam Snyders for nine years and now I am old and have my own home and the Devil is a liar—Glory to God.

For ten or twelve years I traveled through Ontario, Michigan, Indiana and Pennsylvania selling books and Bible's and held meetings and prayermeetings and visited from house to house and the Lord helped me wonderfully and kept me from all harm traveling thousands of miles alone with my Lord.

Hearing it seems me all a wonder when I look back all the way. I found it true all the way what Jesus said that he would give mouth and wisdom that none could gainsay I was much hated and laughed at, but Glory to God I got through without a mark—Praise the Lord O my Soul.

When I was 43 years old the Lord gave me a good young wife. Her name was Jane Blackburn. This made a great uproar. Some laughed and some got mad. Some said, "What will this fellow do with a wife? He cannot support himself. But the Lord made no mistake. It looked very dark to the natural eye. We were married in Penna. then we went to Canada and visited 3 months and had blessed times at Conference and Campmeeting. Praise the Lord O my soul for all His goodness. Then I sold my horse and buckey and sedled all my accounts and paid the fare, then I had 50 dollars and no horse and only a few household artickles and no credit—for people said he is too lazy to work. The reason they said this was because I did so much talk and pray with them. By this they thought to destroy my influence but in the Name of the Lord we began housekeeping—but the Lord did go before. In a short time we had a horse and buckey. The Lord did help in the midst of the enemeys. We had much opposition in our own class in Hatfield but the Lord gave me the victory over all the enemys and over my own self. Glory to God. Self must die before the Lord can have full control.

I was much troubled with Malaria Fever before I got married and afterward I got it every summer. About four years after marriage I got so bad in my bowels I got the conviction that no doctors can help me. I felt to call for the Elders to anoint me as James chap. 5 says. Bro. Wm. Gehman and Bro. Hillegass did anoint me and I had faith and felt happy. After that I went to Royersford to the convention. There the brethren told me I had no faith. They said you will only try it and if the Lord will not help you, you will go back to the doctor. This discouraged me and I went home. Then I thought I would only ask the doctor what my disease is. Then he told me and thought he could help me. He gave me some medicine but I got worse and got melancoly. For three weeks I was in that state. I got tired of the family and every thing and did not know what was the matter.

One evening Bro. Fidler our pastor came in and said this is not the will of God that you sit here. It is the power of darkness and spake with me awhile. Then I could see the wrong I had done in going to the doctor after I was anointed. Then I promised Bro. Fidler to do what God wants me to do. In that intention I went to bed. I was fully given up to live or die and not use a drop of medicine. I could stand firm on the Promise with two feet and had the endurance that the Lord would heal me in that state. I was for six weeks and got worse all the time. When I told others that I would get well, nobody did believe it, even my wife could not believe it because they saw that I got weaker all the time, but the Lord kept me wonderfully. He gave me one promise after another to rest on—Glory to God. My desease worked like consumption. I was not in bed. Some days I was very weak, others I could go out. The last of those weeks I was so weak that they thought I would die soon, but that Sunday morning I got so strong that I could take the train and go to Quakertown to the annual conference and that very day my appitite came. On Thursday when I came home people could see the change and my bowels got healed in a short time—Glory to his Name. It was so evedent and glorious a healing without a drop of medicine that the devil could not gainsay it.

From that time on for about 12 or 13 years I went through all weather, somer and winter to support a large family and the Lord kept me from all harm—praise the Lord O My Soul, for all his goodness. When I got well then we had much to pray. Then the Lord told us to give the tenth to his work and the Sunday eggs to mission work. The devil said it is of no use to do it because it would only make a few dollars, but we began and the Lord Blesses us wonderfully. We could in a short time pay all our debts and from that time till this for 20 years we did lack nothing. We have plenty credit. We had ten children and a good home with plenty of room for meetings and quarterly meetings and came clean through without a scar. The last years the devil tried to pity us for giving so much away, but the more we give the more we get.

About ten years ago I got a weak heart one morning. I was so weak I could not get up. We phoned for Bro. Campbell; he came and anointed me before dinner and the Lord did raise me up and I could go down and take dinner with them— Glory to God. We had much to go through at that time. Four of our children died. The first was a girl of 6 years. We believe she died happy. The next was a baby of 6 weeks. The next was Menno, 17 years of age. He got saved very young. In after years he got in worldly company and backslid. He got sick when he worked away from home and was very bad but got better so that we could take him home, but he was not willing to let go his worldly companions. Then he got worse again. He was sick about 8 weeks. The Lord did not let him die before he had confessed all his sins and left everything. Then he got new life and died very peaceful—Praise the Lord for all his goodness. Great is his love.

The next who died was Jennie, 13 years old. She had three years consumption. She was not as other children for playing. Her whole desire was to serve the Lord. Her delight was to read and sing and pray and praise the Lord. She had much to suffer. Especially the last time. She could hardly wait till the end came. She lived happily and died happy. When I asked her if she would like to get well, she always said just as the Lord will. Before and when Menno was sick, I was again very weak in my heart. The doctor who examined me had no hope for me. One time he did not think I would not live over night and my wife did not know if I or Menno would go first. I did not use no medicine, but when such weak spells came we went on our knees and the power came and the Lord helped every-time—praise his name forever. About 5 years ago when I was at the barn in a moment my heart lost one stroke and since that time it beats only 36 in a minute instead of 72 as it should. I nearly fell down. I had to keep at home about 7 weeks. One year afterwards with that weak heart I got Pheumonia very bad, but the Lord was very near. The spirit spake so sweetly and plain as never before. First he said Peace be still. That sweet voice I shall never forget. I was wonder-fully happy through this sickness. I could not have it when people came in and made a long face. I wanted them to look happy.

This life story was never completed. The writer passed away in 1914—suffer-ing a heart attack. His wife and family were attending the Mizpah Grove Camp-meeting in Allentown. When his wife returned home he failed to come out and assist in tying the horse. She went inside and there beside a huge desk where he often spent long hours in prayer he lay in such a position which clearly indicated he was again having a talk with his Master—and he was not, for God took him.

There was a very large funeral after which meals were served to more than 200 people. His remains are in the small country church yard of an abandoned church building in Montgomery County, Pennsylvania. His wife who passed away in 1938 now rests beside him.

December 25, 1939

JACOB H. MOYER, born October 16, 1842
married Jane Blackburn December 5, 1885
agent for book and medicines

Children:	born	died
Lucy B.	October 1, 1886	Feb. '52
Menno B.	November 17, 1887	4-8-04
Mary B.	November 30, 1888	7-69
William B.	January 24, 1889	Aug. '55
Jennie	June 24, 1893	1-23-07
Lavina	January 2, 1896	2-2-02
Eunice	Dec. 7, 1897	6-8-78
Katie	Nov. 1, 1899	
Sara	Jan. 2, 1902	
Naomi	July 28, 1903	9-8-03

— SON OF —

JACOB L. MOYER, born September 26, 1808, died October 18, 1877
married Sarah Heckler September 22, 1833
She was born February 28, 1816 and died November 28, 1842
He was a farmer - German Baptist
Children - Henry, Elias, Abraham, Aaron, and Jacob

— SON OF —

ABRAHAM MOYER, born Montgomery County March 18, 1786
died May 9, 1866
married Barbara Landis
She was born March 23, 1788, died July 13, 1868
Farmer - Mennonite
Children - Jacob, Henry, Benjamin, Abraham, Katie and Mary

— SON OF —

ABRAHAM MOYER, born December 13, 1767
married Catherine Hagey
Children - Elizabeth, George, Abraham and Susan.

Biographical Sketch of Rev. H. B. Musselman
by Sylvester B. Knerr

The young student of the Bible and famous "boy preacher" was born in Upper Milford, Lehigh County, Penna., on the eleventh day of February, A.D. 1868.

When about four weeks old, he moved with his parents, the venerable Rev. Jonas, deceased, and excellent Christian woman, Mrs. Lucy Musselman, to the town, so familiar to those who have embraced the religion of the founder of this State (Penn)—Quakertown, Bucks County. It was in this village that the lad, or "Little Harvey," as he was commonly known, received his early education. He attended the public schools of the place during the winter months, and in the summer assisted his father, doing chores about the farm. Being of studious and retired habits, Harvey acquired a goodly store of knowledge during these limited school terms of five and six months.

As stated above, his father was a farmer, and an honest, industrious and sober-minded Christian man and minister of the Gospel—a powerful preacher in his day. He was not "slothful in business," but diligent in all things, and on the Lord's Day, he, "fervent in spirit," would proclaim the unsearchable riches of Jesus Christ. The writer is pleased to state that he was privileged to hear him preach several most powerful sermons. Hundreds of souls were brought to Christ and saved through the ministrations of this good man. As a minister, he was sincere and very zealous in the work of the Master.

Mrs. Lucy Musselman, the young man's mother, a woman possessing an enviable moral and Christian character, now an eminent Christian worker, brought up all her children in the fear of the Lord, and with her good influences surrounding Master Harvey, all the better qualities of his boyhood were developed to the noblest and best that the moulding influence of a godly mother can bring to pass. All these things, together with the father's strict rule, for his father was a rigid diciplinarian, rendered invaluable aid in forming the character of this young man.

This young clergyman, beloved by both Jew and Gentile, is often spoken of as being "born a preacher." This we believe to be true, but is possibly due more to his early training than to any other factor, for he was as regular in his attendance at Sunday-school and regular church services as genuine clock-work, rain or shine. He was a boy who "knew his place" on all occasions. As are all boys of worth, so was Harvey possessed of a desire for fun—innocent fun—characteristic of noble boyhood, and his associates were always the respectable class of young men in the neighborhood, but he was rather dignified and conservative in his way, which attracted the attention of the older people generally, and their company was frequently sought.

His bearing was elegant, and he was always careful that his dress was becoming, his hair well brushed, and shoes made to shine like a mirror, in short, the old adage, "Cleanliness is next to Godliness," was evidently a favorite saying with the young man. He often amused his young playmates by "playing preacher," and in this way unconsciously laid the foundation for his future work in the ministry. He was humane in his principles, kind and obedient to his parents, and gracious to all with whom he came in contact.

When twelve years of age it occurred to Harvey that he should like to put some of his knowledge into practice, and concluded that to learn the printing trade would be the best possible way for a boy of his years. He was taken as an apprentice in the printing establishment of Mr. John C. Stauffer, Quakertown. Mr. Stauffer is a very pious gentleman, and under the instruction of so refined a Christian man Harvey learned very rapidly, and by strict attention to this work he soon won the respect of his employer and the other members of the office.

During a leave of absence, granted him in August, 1882, our young printer attended a campmeeting, held at Chestnut Hill, Lehigh County, and while at this place he was convicted of his sins, though only fourteen years of age, and had no rest until he settled the question with his best friend, Jesus. He repented thoroughly of his sins, and Jesus kindly forgave him and cast his sins into the sea of oblivion. He left that camp-ground saying, that "all seemed new to him;" even the rain drops seemed to sparkle with the goodness of God's love, but it was he who had been made a new creature in Christ Jesus, for old things had passed away and all was new. His comrades noticed the change; his life, conduct and conversation all showed clearly that a radical change had taken place, and he never swerved from his purpose. He began to preach to his shopmates, and by his word and example soon influenced his companions for good, and was instrumental in bringing to the Master one who is now the well-known evangelist, C.W. Ruth. He continued faithful and was soon elected Superintendent of the Quakertown Sunday-school of the Mennonite Brethren in Christ. The school flourished amazingly under his supervision, and he became a general favorite with the young and old. He had a kind word for each one of them, and God blessed his labors abundantly.

One of the important points in his life was his call to the ministry. For a long time he tried to conceal it; his agony became more intense, when finally Rev. William Gehman, Sr., at that time Presiding Elder of the Pennsylvania Conference of the Mennonite Brethren in Christ, seeing that there was something troubling the mind of his good boy, which was unusual, he kindly asked him to reveal to him the cause of his anxiety; this he did, and greatly to the relief of his troubled conscience. He was soon given an opportunity to occupy the Quakertown pulpit, and here he preached his first sermon, in 1889, taking for his text, "Mark the perfect man, and behold the upright; for the end of that man is peace," Psalm xxxvii: 37.

He stepped behind the pulpit timidly, for the house was full of people, and in the audience were "some preachers;" but he soon forgot surroundings and the Lord helped him wonderfully insomuch that they all were amazed and stood in wonderment at the eloquence of the "boy preacher."

About this time the reverend gentleman devoted considerable study to the Proverbs of Solomon, and that particular one found in Proverbs xviii: 22, had a peculiar charm for him, yet it was only such as is common to man, and he found his ideal in Miss Annie M. Baus, daughter of Mr. John Baus, of Allentown, whom he wooed and won and was married in holy wedlock, April 23d, 1888. She is a "helpmeet" to him in the true sense of the word; her voice is sweet and clear, just like the dew-drops rolling from the leaves as the sun's morning rays strike them. To them has been born a son, Bryan, who is steadily following in the foot-steps of his father, already well-read in the Holy Bible. This charming little boy was, during his stay at Royersford, a member of the Sunday-school, of which the writer had the honor to be Superintendent for about three years.

At the age of twenty-one, Rev. Musselman moved to Allentown, quitting the printing trade altogether, and devoted his time to the ministry. He was sent from one place to another, preaching the Word, all the time making rapid advances in the good work.

The annual conference of the Mennonite Brethren in Christ, of which he is a member, in 1891 assigned to his charge Royersford, Montgomery County—his first regular appointment. Here his efforts were attended with great success. People flocked to his church from far and near, and it was no unusual occurrence for hundreds to be turned away every evening during protracted meetings or revival services. His church was generally filled by 7 o'clock P.M.

In 1892 he extended his labors to Spring City, Chester County, and was so successful at this place, with the assistance of his helper, Rev. J.B. Knerr, as to be able to build a church the same year. The membership increased steadily; "Many were converted and added to the church." He remained at this place three years, and when the time came for him to depart the people clung to him affectionately, but when they saw that there was no other way, they calmly submitted to the will of God. When he preached his farewell sermon at this place, the house was "packed," and eager crowds listened outside at the open windows. He took for his text, Acts xx: 32, "And now, brethren, I commend you to God, and to the Word of His grace, which is able to bring you up, and give you an inheritance among all them that are sanctified." He held his audience spell-bound for one hour and a half, while he delivered that masterly sermon. The parting scene was sad, as with Paul of old, but the Master called, and he must follow, as he was sent to Weissport, Carbon County, by the sitting of the above-named confer-ence, in 1894.

When Rev. Musselman took charge of Weissport, it was a comparatively small mission; the membership was small, and great opposition prevailed, but in the face of all this he started in a "small upper room," with the full assurance that God would prosper His work, and also give them a more suitable place of worship—a church. He clung to the old ship Zion until she prevailed, and knew nothing but Christ and Him crucified. The language of his heart was: "The Lord will provide." Sinners were converted, backsliders reclaimed and believers sanctified. He went forth heroically like a giant who knows no fear, and as a result of his first year's labor, a church edifice was erected in Weissport and a mission opened in Lehighton. The foundations for a church were laid in Lehighton the same year, but not completed until 1895. He needs no formal introduction, for his work speaks for him.

This young clergyman is the possessor of a bright intellect and vigorous mind; he is an eloquent speaker, and preaches the truth fearlessly; he appears conservative, but is very liberal in his views, yet he adheres strictly to Bible opinions; he is well-versed in Biblical lore, and frequently quotes passage after passage from the Scriptures in his sermons; he is dignified in his bearing, yet possessed of benevolent spirit, and kindness is one of his characteristics. He is a very rapid speaker, yet he is distinct. He often becomes so infatuated with his work as to forget his meals, and it matters not what hour of the night he is called upon to visit and pray with some sick one, a hearty "I'll come," responds to the call, and his presence brings gladness and sunshine to many a weary heart.

May our gracious God and Saviour spare him for many years to come, and make him a blessing to many thousands more, is the prayer of his friend and brother.

Biographical Sketch of Rev. J. B. Knerr
by Sylvester B. Knerr

Jonas B. Knerr, Jr., the youngest son of his father, Jonas Knerr, Sr., deceased, was born in Wessenburg Township, Lehigh County, Penna., February 12th, in the year of our Lord, 1872. His father died in 1890, and his mother is still living, hale and hearty in her old days.

A part of his experience, as related by himself, is given herewith:

"I was growing up to be a very naughty boy. My first school-days were spent in Fogelsville School, Lehigh County. It was here, under the instruction of a good lady teacher, Miss Lichtenwalter, that I learned my A-B-C's, together with many other grand lessons of truth, which still ring in my ears."

The writer remembers many instances of the boys having been invited to the home of this good woman, and, of course, he took advantage of the opportunity. Here some good seed was sown, which afterward sprung up and brought forth abundant fruit. He was always made the recipient of some precious gift from her hand, which naturally increased the friendship of the two.

This little hamlet, Fogelsville, still occupies a precious spot in the memory of the author, not because of the fact of my having spent my first public school days here, but it was my first stepping-stone to Sabbath-school work, having attended an humble Sabbath-school in the village.

Rev. Jonas Knerr, further says: "My teacher loved me, and tried many ways of making me good, but apparently to no avail; I was full of mischief, and did not regard the good, though later on the seed sown sprang forth, and is yielding a rich harvest."

Little Jonas later attended the public schools of Breiningsville, Lehigh County, but here he was retarded in his studies, his teacher having put him from the first reader to the primer. This did not meet with the approval of the lad, for all boys "want to be big," and "Jony" became discouraged, and was not as diligent as formerly.

Later on his parents moved to Seisholtzville, and Master Jonas was again sent to school, but by this time he had acquired a particular dislike for schools, and his teacher tried in vain to keep the boy "straight;" there was "life" in the lad— and he was expelled from school, threatening that he would give that teacher a sound thrashing.

The young man grew; the teacher could do nothing with him at school, and his father concluded to put him to work, but, like a fond indulgent father, never gave him any severe tasks, nor permitted him to work at dangerous places.

At the age of twelve he hired on a farm near Sigmunds, Lehigh County; the people here were very religious, and Jonas stayed only three months and one day. He was now put out to work for his board and clothing, on a farm one mile east of Seisholtzville, Berks County. His master being addicted to the use of tobacco, taught the boy the use of the weed also, as nearly all boys of his age, living in that vicinity, had acquired the habit of chewing and smoking. He says that at this time the Spirit of God strove with him, entreating him to be saved, but he rebelled, and he has often regretted it since, for from that time he went into sin deeper and deeper, seldom thinking of God or eternal things.

In the winter of '85 he made up his mind to do better, and at a revival service, held in Hereford, he came to the altar, experienced a change, but owing to a lack of teaching on a Christian life, he wandered away from God, and in 1886 he hired himself to a farmer near Macungie, Lehigh County, and while here he got into bad company; was taught to play cards, etc., but only when away from his kind master would he and his companions indulge in these evil sports.

He remained at this place two years, and then hired with a farmer near Seisholtzville, where he was so unfortunate as to be so severely injured by the kick of a vicious horse as to render him unconscious for a time. When he came to himself, whom should he find kneeling by his bedside but his good old mother, praying for her boy. This made a lasting impression on his mind. Being of a robust constitution and strong will he soon recovered.

In 1890 he accompanied his parents to Mertztown, where he worked in the ore mines; at eighty cents per day. This was not the best place for the young man, as he came in contact with a very wicked class of people here—miners. The writer knows whereof he speaks, having worked in this place himself. Pay-day was the evil time for these people; whiskey and beer on these days flowed and was drank like water, and the miners, who are very liberal, gave Jonas some of this vile stuff, which he did not refuse. What a sad example of evil companionship! Jonas indulged too freely, and it, of course, acted strangely upon him, for he was not accustomed to beverages of this kind. When he came home dinner was ready, but Jonas could not eat. His mother was at a loss to know what ailed the boy, but soon discovered that he had had "too much," as the saying goes. This caused her great sorrow and distress of mind, but she forgave the poor boy upon his promise to do better.

The theory that a young man *must sow his wild oats,* has no foundation in the Bible, but we have a grand exhortation to the contrary, viz., "Remember thy Creator in the days of thy youth."

The writer at this time lived in Royersford, and, to illustrate a good mother's love, I relate the following: It was in the beautiful month of May, 1890, when the earth was clothed in nature's beautiful green, that I visited the "old folks at home," and when crossing a field near the house, who should I see approaching me but mother; she came running to meet her boy; fell on his neck and kissed him. Father was sitting on the sofa, with his hands over his eyes, but when I entered he welcomed his boy with gladness.

The circumstances surrounding my young brother at the mines, and thinking that it would be better for us all, I made arrangements to bring them to Royersford with me, and we moved to that place on the eleventh day of June.

It was not long after living in this place that Jonas began to attend the grove meetings of the M.B. in C. Church, listened to the glowing testimonials of both old and young, telling of the love of Jesus, and how He saved them, and Jonas came to the conclusion that if these people could enjoy salvation, surely the Lord would save a young sinner like him; he made the step, came to the altar and wept bitterly for his sins; God took notice of him; gave him a new heart, and received him into the kingdom—his name was written in the Book of Life on the twenty-eighth day of June.

This changed the whole course of his life. He now spent his time in reading the Word and storing his mind with Biblical knowledge. Later on he felt the Spirit of God calling him to a more active line of work for the Master; he stated this fact to his pastor, Rev. H.B. Musselman, who asked him to occupy the Royersford pulpit, and he preached his first sermon December 19th, 1892, from the text, Psalm lv: 22, "Cast thy burden upon the Lord, and He shall sustain thee." At this meeting one young lady was persuaded to cast her burden on the Lord, and she has been a true follower of the Lamb ever since.

As a member of the annual conference of the M.B. in C., he was sent, in 1894, as a licensed preacher to take charge of the Coopersburg, Penna., circuit, and at this place he labored in the ministry for one year, with great success, especially at Colesville Mission, where nineteen repented of their sins, accepting Jesus Christ as their full Saviour.

We must not omit an important occurence in this young clergyman's life. Rev. Knerr sought for himself a wife, finding one whom he thought would be a true helpmate to him in all the trials and happinesses of life, Miss Lizzie, a daughter of Samuel P. Kinsell, of White Horse, Schuylkill County, and was joined in the holy bonds of matrimony, February 23d, 1893.

Rev. Jonas Knerr, Jr., is a profound thinker, and possessed of great intellectual faculties, as is clearly indicated by his high noble forehead; a man slow to speak, yet deliberate in his actions; his voice is clear and he is easily understood.

May he always be given up to the service of the Master, is the sincere prayer of his brother.

Rescued From a Miner's Grave
by Sylvester B. Knerr

Jonas B. Knerr, Sr., his wife and family, lived in the vicinity of Fogelsville, Pennsylvania, in the latter half of the nineteenth century. They had three sons: Edwin, Sylvester and Jonas B., Jr. Edwin and Sylvester were involved in an iron mine accident. Edwin died but Sylvester survived to write the following account. Included elsewhere in this book is a biographical sketch of his younger brother, Jonas B., Jr., who became one of the respected pastors of our denomination. His biography of H.B. Musselman gives us insight into the early years of this man of God and former leader of our church. S.B. Knerr's book is significant because it places us into the next generation and introduces us to people, places and the way of life of the early twentieth century.

Editor

CHAPTER I.

Life has its seasons of joy and sorrow, pain and pleasure, tears and triumphs, for every human being. No one has ever lived a life of unalloyed happiness, or been exempted from one or another of the trying circumstances of mortal existence. Several remarkable instances occurring in the life of the writer are submitted herewith.

Just at a time when life seems the fairest, and everything appears correspondingly beautiful, it is frequently, yet sadly, that we are brought into humblest submission. It was a day like this: A bright, beautiful Saturday morning, in the month of June, 1880; the birds sweetly trilling their matins, returning thanks to their Creator; the green meadows, the skipping lambs, the ripening harvests and the crystal air—completed a picture to make a poet sing: "Then, if ever, come perfect days"—that the writer had his first sad experience, which nearly cost his life.

About a mile south of the little town of Brieningsville, in Upper Macungie Township, Lehigh County, Penna., lived, in a little log-house, a poor family, toiling hard, day by day, for their living. The father, Jonas Knerr, Sr., together with two of his sons, worked in an iron-ore bed, for the firm of Lichtenwalter & Butz.

They were poor; but worst of all not looking to their Maker, nor heeding the blessed teachings of His Christ. Nevertheless, God loved them, and sought to win them to Himself, and had a plan by which to do this. These boys were growing into manhood; the oldest, Edwin, being fifteen, and the writer thirteen.

On the day mentioned, we boys left home as usual; full of fun, dinner-kettles filled and in high spirits, thinking not what should befall us that day. Father was working that week in the hay harvest of Mr. Henry Butz, brother to a partner in the mining company. On reaching our destination, we bid our fellow-workmen a pleasant, "Good morning," hitched old Harry, as we called him, to the cart, and were soon driving along, singing merrily.

Oh, how often, as I stand behind the sacred desk and look over the congregation, with its bright faces, it comes to me like lightning that some one of them, or myself, may be called away before the dawn of another day, to meet a just God, who is no respector of persons—to think that we may not meet again in this world. But know this, that we shall meet in the great Beyond, some never to be parted, and some to be separated, brother from sister, mother from daughter, husband from wife, pastor from members. It shall seem wonderful to us that Jesus ever noticed us and saved us for His Kingdom. My dear reader, it was afterward a mystery to me that the Lord so wonderfully saved my life, as I shall presently show you, but now I see the meaning of it all.

We had been working that forenoon, driving to and from the engine house, dumping the loaded cart, and returning for more. I well remember the last load I took up. I had greeted my friend as usual, and was coming down the road, when I met one of my fellow-drivers who had a plan for the noon hour. Some of us boys wanted to take a bath in a mill-dam near by. I drove my cart to the cut, turned the horse around, backed it to the place, and commenced to load. We talked together till the very last minute, thinking of no danger; and the last words my brother said were: "Did you see the Boss?" "Yes," said I, "one of them." We shovelled away, and had the cart about half full of ore, when the bank above us caved in, struck us to the earth and buried us alive with two to four feet of the iron ore covering our bodies. But through it all I was conscious; and when I was being dug out I thought my brother Edwin was helping, not knowing that he lay dead within a few feet of my side. Many have since asked me how I felt and what I was thinking when thus buried out of human sight. We will now endeavor to tell you.

God had His hand in it from beginning to end. While we lay under the earth, no one dreamed that either of us could have been alive; but God was using His spiritual fan upon this poor creature. No human ear heard, but I was crying mightily unto the Lord; and the God of love, whose ear is open to the cry of the needy, sent help out of His Sanctuary on high; but He used human instrumentalities to save me, and to give me another chance to win His favor.

The bank on which we were working was twelve feet high, and a drift or indentation was near-by. As we have said, it was an open cut, and we were using horse and cart when the cave-in occurred. We had started to undermine the bank the day before, and as it was not supported in any way the result was natural. That day is to me as though it had been only yesterday. While I was covered nobody but God saw me, and my whole life came before me as a panorama. All that I ever did stood out before me in great letters. It is of no use for us to try to conceal anything from God. Then I commenced to pray. If you never think of praying during life, you will in the last hours.

If you put it off till then it will almost invariably be too late. Reader, take advice; don't put it off till to-morrow, but to-day, if ye will hear His voice, harden not your hearts. Accept Him now as your Saviour—He came to seek and to save the lost.

And when they uncovered my body, how indescribably grateful I felt to breathe again the pure air, though my body was badly bruised. I looked around and saw that they had just carried the body of my brother to a shady spot. His spirit was gone, his hands and head hanging down, and his head crushed. Oh, pitiful sight! Hundreds of people rushed to the scene and sympathized with the family, and spoke words of comfort to the broken hearts. It may be that some one may read this who has passed through the same experience. Remember that none of our family were Christians at that time; and it was undoubtedly a call of God to us and to the community.

Then kind and good-hearted people laid brother Edwin and myself in a carriage, side by side—he dead, and I badly wounded—and the driver gently drove down the road. May the Lord bless that driver for his care to the wounded boy. When we approached the house, people were crying in great distress. There was sadness and sorrow among the people—and mother especially was in deep agony over the loss of her boy, and the injury to the other.

Mother, you may have lost a dear one; on a sick-bed, perhaps, it was undoubtedly hard for you; but you saw your child dying and could be more easily comforted; it was not so with my mother, for we boys left home in the morning, robust and healthy, and before the clock struck twelve we were brought home— one dead and the other badly wounded. But the Lord of all Grace can comfort under all circumstances. Before they brought us home, the good people rushed to the house to comfort our parents. How welcome they were in that sorrowful hour. Their words were balm to the broken hearts, and the proverb was fulfilled: "A word fitly spoken is like apples of gold in pictures of silver." How true that their hearts were open to receive some truth, and they were drawn nearer to the Lord in that sorrowful hour; but how soon they forgot.

I was laid on my bed for weeks, and then promised the Lord that if he would raise me up I would serve Him to the hour of death. But when He restored my health I soon forgot these vows. I was soon as bad as before; but some good seed had fallen into my heart which was not in vain, as you shall see in the next chapter.

Preparations were made to solemnize the burial of my brother Edwin. On the day appointed, Tuesday, the 23d of June, the remains were taken to and interred in the Fogelsville Cemetery. The funeral sermon was preached by a clergyman of the Reformed Church. The church could not hold the people who came to the service. The preacher selected as his subject an instantaneous death recorded in I Samuel, 20th chapter, and the last part of the third verse: "There is but a step between me and death." It is said that he preached a powerful sermon, but I was not able to be present at the funeral of my own brother.

Dear reader, are you prepared to meet your God! Death, the King of Terrors, will come in an hour that you least expect him.

CHAPTER II.

Life is a reality, beyond doubt; and just "what we make it." How important then that we should give special attention to the make-up of our lives. *Make the tree good, and its fruit will be good.* We are all given a gracious opportunity to do this.

As you have passed over the first chapter you have seen that the writer had a miraculous excape from death. Very truly had Cowper exclaimed:

> "God moves in a mysterious way,
>   His wonders to perform;
> He plants His footsteps in the sea,
>   And rides upon the storm."

God in his infinite mercy spared the writer a little longer; for, in that dreadful hour, he was not prepared to meet his God. I was spared for a purpose. God sees and knows the secret intents of a man's heart, and so spoke to the writer when buried alive, as it were. It was not the first time. Five years before when swimming I narrowly escaped death, being rescued by a young companion. Some Scripture references may serve to illustrate my sad experiences: "And the word of the Lord came unto Jonah the *second* time," Jonah iii:I, "For God speaketh once, yea *twice*, yet man perceiveth it not. In a dream, in a vision of the night, when deep sleep falleth upon men, in slumberings upon the bed; then he openeth the ears of men, and sealeth their instruction that he may withdraw man from his purpose, and pride from man. He keepeth back his soul from the pit, and his life from perishing by the sword." Job xxxiii: 15-18.

Dear reader, perhaps you have passed through a similar experience. You may still be spared, but it is for a purpose; to perform some work for the Master; to be in a position to be used for His cause. You who have passed through great trouble and sorrow, you are spared to do some special work in the Master's vineyard. The men most used to-day are generally those who have passed through the school of tribulation and correction. Such men can be more used because they can better feel for the woes of fallen humanity. As God has said, through the prophet of old, "I have chosen thee in the furnace of affliction." When His children are in the furnace of affliction He shall sit as a refiner and purifier of silver, and when the dross is consumed He shall know it, and use you to perform some of His great and marvelous works. Little do we know when young, where

94

God will lead us. Then let us have the motto, "Where He leads I will follow," and let us show perfect obedience to him, for then we have the promise to eat of the good of the land. Great is the goodness of God. If we had a thousand tongues we could not express His goodness and love toward us. He hath loved us with an everlasting love; with loving kindness He hath drawn us to Himself, and we can clearly say with Solomon: "His banner over me is love."

When covered with the earth and ore, all thought that both of us were smothered, and they were greatly astonished that I was still alive. But, as I have said, God, by His holy angels, took care of me. With God all things are possible. Jonah was in the whale's belly three days and three nights, but when he cried to the Lord, "the Lord spake unto the fish, and it vomited out Jonah upon the dry land." The experience of the writer was, in a sense, similar to this. "I cried unto the Lord by reason of mine affliction, and He heard me." God sent deliverance in due time to save my life. It took an amount of crying; but, nevertheless, He whose ear is not heavy and whose arm is not shortened, heard and answered prayer so as to be the most effective and beneficial.

These pages are not written for vain glory, but simply to show what God does for humanity, and what He can and will do for His creatures. He uses various ways in bringing His lost sheep into the fold. May the God of Heaven open the eyes and ears of every one who reads these facts. The poet has well said:

"His purposes will ripen fast,
    Unfolding every hour;
The bud may have a bitter taste,
    But sweet will be the flower."

God does not force any one to Himself, but invites and warns and waits. Then be submissive to His gentle voice, and you will be irresistibly drawn to the Lamb of God, which taketh away the sin of the world. But some one may ask why such rough means are used for some and more ordinary and quiet means for others. God is Master of ways and knows all things best. Some time, if not now, you will realize that truly all things have worked for your good, whether rough or smooth.

"Judge not the Lord by feeble sense,
    But trust Him for His grace;
Behind a frowning providence
    He hides a smiling face."

In those dark hours the Lord was there smiling upon His son. His voice was heard, saying, "Fear not, it is I; be of good cheer, and I will show you the way of salvation." So, in such an hour, it is only to hold still and see the salvation of the Lord.

That hour was a dark one to me, but at the same time one of the most instructive of my life. The beautiful sun of the blessed Gospel commenced to shine into my darkened, miserable heart. Though I was young, yet the seed was sown, and four years later it began to spring up. I attended the revival services in St. John's

95

Church, Hereford, Berks County, Penna., held by the Rev. Abel Strawn, of the M.B. in C. Church. As he was preaching the Gospel, the writer was convinced of his sin, came to the altar, repented and embraced the religion of the Lord Jesus, which has kept him to the present day. "And I am persuaded that he is able to keep that which I have committed unto him against that day."

It is a very easy matter to turn to the Lord and seek salvation; but often hard for people to believe that Jesus will so convert the soul as to change our vile nature and to fashion it according to His own divine nature. Most people do not believe this, but the simple, trustful soul just believes every word, and so obtains the blessing.

"If our love were but more simple,
We should take Him at His word;
And our lives would be all sunshine
In the sweetness of our Lord."

My prayer to God, is that, if the reader has not surrendered his will to the divine will and appropriated the promises of God by simple faith, now shall be the time.

As you have seen, the Lord Jesus became my portion when but a boy. But not having the teaching which babes in Christ should have, I became cold and fell into a backslidden state, where so many are to-day, not knowing that they have lost their first love. A few years after, however, I started afresh with more zeal and energy than ever; commenced to read the German Bible, and my soul was again blessed of God.

Every minister of the Gospel should teach his young converts the use of the blessed Bible which is able to make them wise unto salvation. He then has the assurance that they will grow in grace and in the knowledge of our Lord and Saviour Jesus Christ. The Christian should make it a point to use the Scriptures as the pre-eminent Lamp to his feet, and Light to his path.

"Oh the Bible, blessed Bible!
God's truth revealed in its pages.
It strengthens the young and it comforts the old;
It stands like a rock through the ages."

And surely, in studying the Bible, they will never be led astray. Why? Because they have hid the Word of God in their hearts, therefore they cannot sin against him.

When a man is soundly converted, the hunger and thirst for the living Word, the Bread of Life, is imparted to the soul; and the desire is always to know more about Jesus. The way to learn more about Him is through His blessed Word. Jesus Himself said, "Search the Scriptures; for in them ye think ye have eternal life; and they are they which testify of Me," John v: 39. And again: "If any man will do His will he shall know of the doctrine, whether I speak of myself," John vii: 17. A true Christian's delight is in the earnest reading of the Word, and such an one is much used in the Master's vineyard. It will be his very delight to meditate on the law of the Lord day and night, as the Psalmist has said. Such an one will grow in grace; and people will take notice that he belongs to the little band which is not easily discouraged, but which is steadily going onward and upward, and at last will sweep through the everlasting portals never to return, but to meet on the shining shores where sorrow and sighing shall flee away and where the redeemed shall be forever with the Lord.

God knows what is in man and foresees in what way he can use him best. His days are numbered, and after all they are but few. Just time enough to do our mission below and prepare for the world to come. He is sowing the seed in apparently desolate and waste ground, but then He causes the bud of the tender herb to spring forth. To some it may seem long coming, but in due season it will spring up. *Mother's prayers will be answered.* Not a holy desire breathed forth in prayer shall be lost, but in His own good time it shall be done to us according to our faith. He is always the best friend in time of need. So, when the billows roll over us, let us fly to Jesus, for refuge and strength.

> "The raging storms may round us beat,
>   A shelter in the time of storm;
> We'll never leave our safe retreat,
>   A shelter in the time of storm."

Is Jesus all this to you in time of trouble? Then let us hide in the rock; "In the rock that is higher than I," and we will never be disappointed. For, if we meet what is usually called disappointment and term it, "His-appointment," He will surely satisfy with goodness the longing of the soul.

There is a time when men think they have no need of God—when all is going smoothly; when in prosperity and good health. So he is without God and remains an alien to the Commonwealth of Israel. But God still loves him and brings him to a halt, because it is not His will that any soul should perish, but would have all men to be saved and come to the knowledge of truth. Therefore, with some He must use the rod of affliction to draw them from destruction and to holy things. When you are sorely afflicted it does not seem sweet nor the work of a loving hand. But then is the time to stop and consider:

> "The bud may have a bitter taste,
>   But sweet will be the flower."

Dear reader, you may have passed through such an experience; no doubt it was bitter at first, but if you have been submissive, the opening of the flower was sweet.

We are apt to become morbid if we brood too long over our troubles, and think we alone have had the afflicting hand laid upon us, but by looking about us we find that others, too, are scouraged. In one of my visits a dear old mother related to me an occurrence as sad as the event which befell our home. Her boy, years before, had left his home in the morning well, but before sunset was brought home dead. As she related this to me the tears coursed down her cheeks; and the blessed words of the Psalmist came to my mind: "They that sow in tears shall reap in joy. He that goeth forth and weepeth, bearing precious seed, shall doubtless come again with rejoicing, bringing his sheaves with him." So we find that such tears as these are not lost but, as David saith, they are bottled.

Well do I remember, when in agony of spirit, I cried unto the Lord, He heard me. The God of infinite compassion in mercy delivered His son from the horrible pit.

Many friends have asked me as to how I felt when covered by the cold earth. At first it was dark, oh, how dark! But as I commenced to pray there shone a ray of light into my poor benighted heart; and then soon they brought me to the pure air again. But oh, how sad I felt to know that my dear brother was dead—the one I had loved so dearly, to be so suddenly snatched from my side, and to be called to that long eternity beyond. I shall never forget that dying hour of my brother. Yet God was in it all, for I was warned to flee from the wrath to come, and my brother was taken where no night shall come, but endless noon and joy unspeakable. And shall we not soon be gathered home, too?

"When at last to our home we gather
With the loved ones gone before
We will sing on that happier shore,
Praising Him for His love evermore."

Then we will say, the best friend to have is Jesus, in life or in death. Thanks be to God for the knowledge that those who are one the way are journeying to a home above, "where sorrow and sighing shall flee away, where the wicked shall cease from troubling and the weary are at rest."

"No night shall be in heaven; no gathering gloom
Shall o'er that glorious landscape ever come.
No tears shall fall in sadness o'er those flowers
That breathe their fragrance through celestial bowers.
No night shall be in heaven; forbid to sleep:
These eyes no more their mournful vigils keep;
Their fountains dried, their tears all wiped away,
They gazed, undazzled, on eternal day.
No night shall be in heaven; no sorrow reign.
No secret anguish, nor corporeal pain,
No shivering limbs, no burning fevers there,
No soul's eclipse, no winter of despair.
No night shall be in heaven, but endless noon;
No fast declining sun, no waning moon;
But there the Lamb shall yield perpetual light,
Mid pastures green and waters ever bright.
No night shall be in heaven; no darkened room,
No bed of death, nor silence of the tomb.
But breezes ever fresh with love and truth
Shall brace the frame with an immortal youth.
No night shall be in heaven; but night is here,
The night of sorrow, and the night of fear

I mourn the ills that now my steps attend,
And shrink from others that may yet impend.

No night shall be in heaven. Oh, had I faith
To rest in what the faithful witness saith,
That faith should make these hideous phantoms flee,
And leave no night henceforth on earth to me."

Kind reader, if you are on the Lord's side, look to Him for your strength, and make the Bible the man of your counsel, and by so doing you will be prosperous on your Christian journey. And you who are not His, turn ye, turn ye! As the prophet saith! "Look unto Me, and be ye saved, all the ends of the earth; for I am God, and there is none else."

CHAPTER III.

The heavens declare the glory of God, and the firmament showeth His handiwork. The earth may crumble to dust; the stars may cease to shine in the heavens, and though the sun and moon refuse to send their glittering rays through aerial space, the goodness of the Lord will remain the same, and His mercy endure forever.

You have already seen how wonderfully gracious the Lord was to the writer. In a dangerous place, how short-sighted we are! It is only when we have passed that point that we see the hand of the guardian angel. But God knows all things best, and in order to draw us to Himself He often has to use the rod of affliction. Oh, then, beloved, let us fly to His loving breast in the time when all is well and favorable—when we can give our fullest powers and our best service. There is a special promise to the young: "I love them that love Me and those that seek Me early shall find Me." As we know these things let us attend to them at once, departing from all evil and cleaving to that which is good. Then you shall be rich toward God, think of it! You shall say with David: "Surely goodness and mercy shall follow me all the days of my life, and I will dwell in the house of the Lord forever.

The *lesson of life* is obedience to God. Alas, how few have learned it; but those who have can say truly that obedience is grand, and the fruit thereof is lasting sweetness. And what of disobedience? Is not the result always sadness, gloom, and a troubled spirit? Have we not all more or less shown disobedience in our past life, and has not the fruit been bitter? At first it may not appear to be so, but remember it will come as sure as darkness follows day. But, thanks be to God, we are invited to return, and He will abundantly pardon; return to give the Master loyal service and loving obedience. And, if we are willing and obedient we shall eat of the good of the land.

By nature, we are all inclined to disobey and to be rebellious; but, praise His dear name, He has promised to change our vile natures, and to fashion us according to His own divine nature. Isn't it a glorious heritage? Our stubborness will He forgive and cast all our sins into the sea of oblibion, never to remember them against us any more forever. For, as by one man's disobedience many were made sinners, so by the obedience of one shall many be made righteous. So there is hope for you and me, if we will only accept the proffered salvation.

Through disobedience we have fallen into trouble, misery and darkness. Then we say: "If we had only known that this would have been the end, how differently we would have done." Disobedience leads to bondage, and at last to the perdition of hell. Then hope is gone. Friend, rouse from your sleep and serve the true God! That alone brings true happiness in time and eternity. So shall your light shine more and more unto the perfect day. Your path will shine with the light of heaven, and the angels of God will whisper comfort to your soul. Your life will be a blessing, and your influence a benediction. Jesus Himself will make His abode in your heart. Then, beloved, let us adopt the rule of perfect obedience. Your children and your children's children will rise up and call you blessed. Jesus will bless you and anoint your head with oil of gladness, and truly your cup shall run over. Many shall be blessed by your life, and when the end comes it will only be to fall asleep in Jesus, "blessed sleep, from which none ever wake to weep." "Blessed are the dead which die in the Lord from henceforth; yea, saith the Spirit; that they may rest from their labors; and their works do follow them."

By which route will you go? Reader, take the Gospel route, which is obedience; so your testimony will be: "The joy of the Lord is my strength." If you have that joy then you are strong; if you are spiritually weak, it is because you are destitute of the joy resultant from faithful service. When you were first converted, all was bright and joyous, and you were willing to do anything for the Master. But you had just entered the school.

Presently the Master brought before you a clear vision of the work you were to do, but it was apparently too hard. You refused, saying: "Somebody else can do it better than I." Take care! This is the first step in disobedience. Remember, nobody else can do your work. This man or that brother may be more talented for the work, but the Lord wants to lead you out in the way of obedience. They have grown in grace and you must grow, by implicit obedience.

> "We have no wings, we cannot soar;
>   But we have feet to scale and climb
> By slow degrees, by more and more,
>   The cloudy summits of out time.
>
> The heights by great men reached and kept
>   Were not attained sudden flight,
> But they, while their companions slept,
>   Were toiling upward in the night.
>
> Standing on what we too long bore
>   With shoulders bent and downcast eyes,
> We may discern—unseen before—
>   A path to higher destinies."

Take courage then, brother, sister; there is something good in store for you. No matter how insignificant, or how difficult, without questioning, commit thy way unto the Lord, and He shall prosper thee.

You may think yourself called of God to preach His Gospel. But are you willing to work at home? Do you say, "There is nothing for me to do at home?" Why, bless your soul, there is something everywhere for you to do. A seeking for preeminence in the work is a frequent hindance—lookout for it! A person with the working spirit within him is the busiest, and God is using such every day, to His glory. There is room for any number of workers. We cannot all go out into the mission fields at home or abroad, but we can all work, and do our share right where we are. The greatest preachers in the eyes of God are those of perfect obedience.

Education is not a vital factor in walking with God, or showing to our fellow-men a bright example, which is the most effectual preaching.

A washerwoman may walk before God as a queen, and before men as an example, though her prayers be ungrammatical and her testimonies halting and broken.

"To obey is better than sacrifice." How true the writer has found this in his experience. When first converted he felt called to preach the Gospel; but by disobedience he grew cold in faith. Like Moses of old he had many excuses to offer; he had a stammering tongue and no apparent ability for the office and work of the ministry. At first he did not obey the gentle voice of the Spirit, but God presently brought it about in a most mysterious manner. His word was, "Go, I will be with thee." Bless God, I then obeyed, took the Gospel trumpet, and went on the Lord's mission. He has helped me, and where He leads I will follow.

Dear reader, permit me to urge you to obey the Holy Spirit. There are many spirits gone out trying to deceive, if possible, the very elect. But try the spirits; if they correspond with the Word, then are they of God. First, know that you are prompted of the Holy Spirit, then follow at once. Stand by your colors; stand for righteousness. Do right, for the sake of Him who is righteous; and the smiles of the Lord shall beam upon you in streams of infinite complacency; you shall receive the approbation of men, and the portals of glory shall afford you an abundant entrance, to the City of God, where you shall be made the recipient of a crown of glory, which fadeth not away.

Treatise on Ephesians VI: 1-3
by S. B. Knerr

"Children, obey your parents in the Lord; for this is right. Honor thy father and mother; which is the first commandment with promise; that it may be well with thee, and thou mayest live long on the earth."

There never was an age or period of time when opportunities for acquiring knowledge were as great as at the present time—they are golden; let us take advantage of them. The times of ignorance have passed, and God winked at them, but now he commands all to search the Scriptures; be diligent in the study of the Word, and enrich the mind with the best this age affords.

God has given certain talents to all, and we are to utilize them to the best possible advantage. The plea of ignorance is of no consequence to-day; the opportunities are too great. "Ignorance of the law excuses no one." We are all born into the world for some purpose. It is true we do not all have equal prosperity, but this is not the fault of the Creator; the blame rests upon the creature, and very often it is due to disobedience on the part of the unfortunate.

The Lord is always willing to help an honest, obedient person. Obedience is first learned in the home. The child who is obedient to his parents, will have the divine benediction resting upon it, and grow up to be a man after God's own heart.

Obedience to parents is a divine command, and there are many promises attendant upon a compliance with the blessed injunction. You will be sure of a happy life here—of both temporal and spiritual things shall you receive from the hands of God most liberally. "It will go well with thee." Solomon says, "The eye *that* mocketh at *his* father, and despiseth to obey *his* mother, the ravens of the valley shall pluck it out, and the young eagles shall eat it." Many young men and women are eaten up, and they are not aware of the sad fact, some are in this state at twenty-five, some at eighteen, and even younger.

I have an instance in my mind of a god-fearing mother, Mrs. Peters, of Fogelsville, Lehigh County. Her husband fell asleep in Jesus when quite young, and the widow was left to struggle alone, having three little boys to support, the eldest being five years of age.

This good woman raised these boys for the Lord, and in turn they loved and obeyed her, as children should, and all three are now ministers of the Gospel; we make special mention of the eldest, Dr. Madison C. Peters, the brilliant New York orator, and prominent lecturer of the day, who is known all over the United States, the writer himself speaking of them from an intimate personal acquaintance with the three boys. There were no boys, to my knowledge, who showed a more marked obedience to their widowed mother, and her instructions fell like the dew from heaven into the hearts of these boys, and note the result—thousands have arisen and called these men blessed.

This law of obedience is divine, yet it may be applied to all callings in life. Train up a child in the right way, and he will grow up right. This was proved in the case of the three boys just spoken of. Mrs. Peters taught her children to obey her commandments, for she took the Bible as her guide in all things. The boys were taught early to pray to Him who hears the supplications of the needy, and as a result of this careful training their fame as preachers, is now spread broadcast over the world.

Therefore, children, if you would have it go well with you, obey your parents in the Lord, and in turn God will bless you and men will praise you, and justly so; for "a good name," which is earned by a righteously obedient life, "is rather to be chosen than great riches."

The Upper Milford Mennonite Church.

Known as the "Nummer Zwei" (Number two) Church, Zionsville, Pennsylvania.

This restored photo is the only known picture of the meeting house where Wm. Gehman, Wm. N. Shelly and others worshipped before they were put out of that conference and formed the Evangelical Mennonites in 1858.

William Gehman - 1827-1918.
The founder of the Bible Fellowship Church.

Zionsville Bible Fellowship Church.

The first church of the denomination. Founded in 1858 has been an active church for 125 years.

NINITE MEETIN HOUSE

Calvary Bible Fellowship Church, North Main Street, Coopersburg, Pennsylvania, the second church of the denomination. This building was used for worship until 1967 when a new building was built adjoining it. The "Old Mennonite Meeting House" still stands as a testimony to those early years.

David Musselman

The picture of David Musselman on the lef
belonged to H.B. Musselman.

An inscription on the back states "Grandfathe
David Musselman — a most beautiful Chris
tian."

The picture below was taken when he was 95
reading his beloved Bible without glasses. He
died November 21, 1904, at the age of 96 years
6 months and 12 days.

David Musselman's Farm, Dillingersville, Pennsylvania. The farm house where the first conference was held in 1858.

Believed to be the oldest picture in the archives
of the Historical Committee... This picture in-
cludes W.B. Musselman and A.B. Gehret. The
other men have not been identified.

My Likeness

My likeness some would like to see,
Read careful all the poetry,
In righteousness and holiness,
God made man in his own likeness.

How far I imitate within
My Maker who hates every sin,
I must to those around me give;
Such a photograph does live.

Those which mortal man can take,
The outside, that's the body's shape:
Mine hangs not yet on any wall,
I never may have such a call.

My outward likeness I can meet,
If I look right beneath my feet.
Each one's body soon must lay,
In the dust, so God doth say.

Some dress stylish, very nice,
And have their likeness taken twice:
By such the soul neglected is,
While they seek not for heavenly bliss.

This subject I will not make long,
In other matters I am throng;
I'll have to hasten to a close,
The truth so pointed will make foes.

Your face I here may never see,
If you're a Christian, pray for me,
In grace and knowledge let us grow,
In piety, our likeness show.

Eusebius Hershey

No photograph is known to exist of Hershey, but these verses from his own pen present an excellent "image" of this man of God.

General Conference at Berlin, Ontario - 1900
Front (seated) H. Pontius, P.E.   J.C. Hallman
Row 1 - C.K. Curtis, A. Good, I. Pike, H.S. Hallman, Sec., C.H. Brunner, Pres.
P. Cober, P.E., H. Goodie, P.E., S. Eby
Row 2 - J. Buzzard, H.S. Wismer, S. Lambert, W.G. Gehman, S.B. Schneider,
H.B. Musselman, W.B. Musselman, M.P.E., O.B. Snyder, P.E., A. Wright
Row 3 - J.G. Shireman, O.B. Henderson, D. Brenneman, P.E., M. Bowman, E.
Anthony

Canada	Indiana & Ohio	Pennsylvania	Iowa & Nebraska
Cober	Brenneman	Brunner	Pontius
Goodie	Good	H.B. Musselman	Henderson
Bowman	Lambert	W.B. Musselman	
Eby	Wright	W.G. Gehman	
H.S. Wismer	Buzzard	Shireman	Michigan
Pike		A.A. Wismer	O.B. Snyder
Scheider		(not in photo)	Anthony
			Hallman

This rare picture portrays both Soloman Ebe of
Ontario, and Daniel Breneman of Indiana, who
were leaders of the United Mennonites. It was
taken in 1900 at the General Conference in Berlin
(now Kitchner) Ontario, Canada.

The Board of Foreign Mission in 1911.

H.B. Musselman (seated left), Wm. Gehman (standing left), Allan M. Gehman (standing center), E.N. Cassel (standing right), C.H. Brunner (seated right).

At the turn of the century a new generation of church leaders began to appear, and new names were heard.

As the denomination grew so did its activities. This was recorded at the Sunday School Convention at Coopersburg Church in 1902.

The Gospel Workers Society, a society of women only was recognized in 1898. Door to door visitation, and selling "The Gospel Herald" was a major part of their daily ministry.

The Gospel Herald Society, for men only, was founded in 1899 by C.H. Brunner. This society existed to train new ministers and open new churches.

Annual Conference. Mennonite Brethren in Christ Church, 10th and Oley Street, Reading, Pennsylvania. October 10-15, 1906.

Front Row (left to right) L.B. Taylor, W Hottel, J.G. Shireman, E.T. Schick, F Musselman, W.G. Gehman, C.H. Brun E.N. Cassel, J.C. Roth, J.F. Barrall, W Gehman

ond Row: C.J. Edwards, P.J. Musselman, R.L. Woodring, E.E. Kublic, G.A. Campbell, W. Steinmetz,
. Hillegas, R. Bergstresser, C.W. Stine, L. Frank Haas, Third Row: J.A. Kern, F.P. Brobst, W.D. Evert,
. Musselman, H.F. Meltzer, W.J. Fretz, Allen M. Gehman, G.O. Billig, M.M. Ziegler, Fourth Row:
. Teel, E.R. Hartman, Adam Keller R.D. Hollenbach, O.C. Kistler, B. Engelman, H.H. Bergey, G.K.
nmelreich, Leidy Sell, J.M. Oplinger.

H.B. Musselman

The boy preacher.

Presiding Elder.

Wm. G. Gehman Family

Wm. G. Gehman

Edgewood Camp Meeting, Shamokin,
Pennsylvania.

Camp Meeting — a highlight of chur
activity.

Mizpah Grove — Believed to be about 1912.

Mizpah Grove,
Allentown,
Pennsylvania,
1916.

Literature Tent, Mizpah Grove, Allentown. Pa.

Group in front of tent.
Wm. Gehman (second
from left.)

For many years Tent Meetings and Revival Meetings were the method of evangelistic outreach.

E.N. Cassel and his horse Captain.

From the old horsepower . . .
to a new horsepower.

H.B. Musselman with E.N. Cassel and family.

Coopersburg Mennonite Brethren in Christ Church in 1930.

H.B. Musselman.

The Gospel Herald Society in 1937 taken at the Jersey City Mission.

Front Row: Eugene George, J.T. Anderson, W. Bruce Musselman, W.G. Gehman, E.J. Rutman, E.W. Bean

Standing: George Watson, Jim Hean, John Golla, Jack Dunn, Paul Schuler, R.C. Reichenbach, Tom Turnbull, C.E. Kirkwood, J.F. Sommers.

Back Row: E.F. Lakjer, Mervin Ruth, Tommy Thompson, D. Foreman.